Shakespeare's Tragicomic Vision

Shakespeare's Tragicomic Vision

JOAN HARTWIG

Louisiana State University Press
BATON ROUGE

ISBN 0-8071-0047-1
Library of Congress Catalog Card Number 79-181567
Copyright © 1972 by Louisiana State University Press
All rights reserved
Manufactured in the United States of America
Printed by The TJM Corporation, Baton Rouge, Louisiana
Designed by Dwight Agner

Chapter IV appeared in slightly different form as "The Tragicomic Perspective of *The Winter's Tale*" in *ELH*, XXXVII (March, 1970), 12-36, © 1970 by The Johns Hopkins Press.

To Mother and Dad

ACKNOWLEDGMENTS

I wish to thank Professor Lawrence J. Ross for encouraging me to be a member of Shakespeare's audience without anachronistic guilt. His careful reading of the first draft of this book and the incisive commentary which he gave me have been of the greatest value. I would also like to express my gratitude to Professors Robert Buffington, Joseph H. Summers, and Aubrey L. Williams, who have been kind enough to read and comment upon the manuscript at later stages, and to Florida State University for a summer grant that helped my revisions.

CONTENTS

Shakespeare's Tragicomic Vision

Chapter I ❧ THE EXPLORATION
OF A GENRE

Toward the end of his career Shakespeare began to work with a new kind of play. *Pericles, Cymbeline, The Winter's Tale,* and *The Tempest* form a cohesive group distinct from the rest of the canon despite the fact that parts of them resemble other Shakespearean plays. Apparently they were all written within a period of five years between 1606 and 1611.[1] Shakespeare was writing other plays at the same time, of course, so that dates alone are insufficient cause for grouping these plays together.[2] The dates suggest, however, that Shakespeare was beginning to develop during these years a new kind of play markedly different from the other genres in which he had achieved success.[3] All four plays

[1] See J. Leeds Barroll, "The Chronology of Shakespeare's Jacobean Plays and the Dating of *Antony and Cleopatra*," in G. R. Smith (ed.), *Essays on Shakespeare* (University Park, Pa., and London, 1965), 115–62; E. K. Chambers, *William Shakespeare: A Study of Facts and Problems* (2 vols.; Oxford, 1930), I, 271; and James G. McManaway, "Recent Studies in Shakespeare's Chronology," *Shakespeare Survey*, III (1950), 22–33.

[2] According to Chambers' dating, the following plays were being composed in the same period: *King Lear* (1605–1606); *Macbeth* (1605–1606); *Antony and Cleopatra* (1606–1607); *Coriolanus* (1607–1608); *Timon of Athens* (1607–1608).

[3] *Pericles* was entered in the Stationers' Register on May 20, 1608, to-

contain similar story materials: a royal child is lost and re-discovered; sea journeys change men's lives; scenes occur in different countries, most of them remote; the main characters struggle against adversity and are rewarded in the end; characters thought dead are miraculously resurrected; and the final reconciliation is achieved through the agency of young people. Certain thematic patterns emerge from these materials, and the attempt to isolate the significance of these patterns has led many critics to interpret the plays as myths, as symbols, or as allegories.[4] In each play the main characters

gether with *Antony and Cleopatra*, and F. D. Hoeniger speculates that it was composed between 1606 and 1608; see Arden edition, *Pericles* (London, 1963), lxiii–lxv. J. Leeds Barroll concurs with Hoeniger's discussion and suggests that his own argument for the dating of *Antony and Cleopatra* supplements Hoeniger's for *Pericles*; see Barroll, "The Chronology of Shakespeare's Jacobean Plays," 162 n. 71. J. M. Nosworthy suggests that *Cymbeline* and *The Winter's Tale* may have been composed simultaneously, probably during 1608–1609, when the plague had prohibited acting in London; see Arden edition, *Cymbeline* (London, 1964), xvi–xvii. Simon Forman's record of having seen performances of both plays before April, 1611, limits the forward date, and most critics accept E. K. Chambers' dating of the plays, which places *Cymbeline* about 1609–10 and *The Winter's Tale* 1610–11. According to the Revels Accounts, *The Tempest* was presented at court in 1611, which is its first recorded performance. Since the Office of the Revels may have selected old plays as well as commissioned new ones, this record does not mean that *The Tempest* had not been performed earlier. Frank Kermode points out, however, that *The Tempest* "uses material not available until the latter part of 1610, and Simon Forman, who saw, among other plays at the Globe, *Cymbeline* and *The Winter's Tale*, apparently did not see *The Tempest* there"; see Arden edition, *The Tempest* (London, 1966), xxii. Therefore, despite the speculative dating of each play, *Pericles* is probably the first and *The Tempest*, the last of the group. The order of composition becomes important in arguments that attempt to demonstrate a progressive development in the handling of similar materials. My purpose is not primarily to show such a development, but the evidence seems to support it. I have arranged my discussions of the individual plays according to the order of composition indicated here.

4 For example, D. G. James, "The Failure of the Ballad Makers," in *Scepticism and Poetry* (New York, 1960), 233, thinks that Shakespeare's primary myth of resurrection failed him because it was "inadequate to his purpose." G. Wilson Knight, *The Crown of Life* (London, 1965), 30, views the plays as "myths of immortality . . . parables of a profound and

aspire toward some perfect relationship; that hope is shattered; and finally the original wish is fulfilled in a manner which leaves the characters amazed.

The amazement is not restricted to the characters in the play. The audience, too, experiences a sense of wonder that the events presented to them could in any way be believed. As the plays affirm that which we know cannot be true, we feel a peculiar dislocation, a sense of being manipulated into a paradoxical response, at once involved and critically distant from the action. For example, in *The Winter's Tale*, we are sympathetically involved in Antigonus' dilemma when he is forced to abandon Perdita on the shore of Bohemia. Suddenly the bear appears and chases Antigonus off the stage (III.iii.58). This action is likely to create laughter, and the laughter creates a distance between the dramatic action and the audience's involvement in it. At this distance, we realize what we have been laughing at—the enactment of death—and we experience a startling dislocation. The old Shepherd and the Clown channel our response immediately; but, for that brief moment, assumed values have been shaken. As Bonamy Dobrée puts it, "Shakespeare seems to—what shall I say?—sport with us, till he frees us finally in a kind of exalted relief."[5] The sporting quality of the last plays derives from a heavy stress on artifice, and this stress forces the audience to see the art as art, disallowing a false fusion between art and life. Toward the end of the play we seem to find that the two disparate worlds have merged; yet when we leave the theater they separate again. In the process we

---

glorious truth." Derek Traversi, *Shakespeare: The Last Phase* (Stanford, Calif., 1955), 2, 18, sees the plays as "expanded images" which move toward rebirth and reconciliation. See Philip Edwards' review of this kind of critical approach, "Shakespeare's Romances: 1900–1957," *Shakespeare Survey*, XI (1958), 6–12.

[5] Bonamy Dobrée, "The Last Plays," in Robert Gittings (ed.), *The Living Shakespeare* (London, 1960), 145.

have experienced the unique pleasure of having our imaginations touched and revitalized.

Not all spectators or readers of these plays feel this pleasure, of course; and it is interesting to notice that those who dislike or dismiss the plays usually do so because they disapprove of the stress on artifice. Ben Jonson discounted *Pericles* as a "mouldy tale," [6] and Samuel Johnson dismissed *Cymbeline* because of its absurd artificiality: "To remark the folly of the fiction, the absurdity of the conduct, the confusion of the names and manners of different times, and the impossibility of the events in any system of life, were to waste criticism upon unresisting imbecillity [*sic*], upon faults too evident for detection, and too gross for aggravation." [7] Harley Granville-Barker has answered Johnson's energetic dismissal with a perceptive explanation of why the art "displays its art"; but he too finds that the technique "is a thing very likely to be to the taste of the mature and rather wearied artist." [8] Lytton Strachey's well-known criticism that Shakespeare was "bored . . . with everything except poetry and poetical dreams" accounts for the obviousness of the artifice as mere indifference to the problems of construction. [9] Bertrand Evans is only one of many who object to the crudities of stagecraft in *Pericles*: he thinks a device like Gower is "unworthy" of Shakespeare. [10] Distaste for obvious artifice is at the core of most of the detractors' criticisms, and it implies a rather puritanical resistance to the sense of

[6] See Ben Jonson's poem "Ode to Himselfe," lines 21–22.

[7] [Samuel Johnson], *Johnson on Shakespeare*, ed. Walter Raleigh (London, 1952), 183.

[8] Harley Granville-Barker, *Prefaces to Shakespeare*, Second Series (3 vols.; London, 1927–36), II, 244–47.

[9] Lytton Strachey, "Shakespeare's Final Period," in *Books and Characters* (London, 1928), 50.

[10] Bertrand Evans, *Shakespeare's Comedies* (Oxford, 1960), 223.

"play" which allows us to observe ourselves at the same time we are undergoing an imaginative and emotional experience. It is not necessarily "decadent" to create such a critical perspective, although many critics imply that it is. The double awareness of being simultaneously involved and removed is not a matter of being "toyed with" by the playwright for the mere exploitation of the method. It directs us toward an ethical reassessment of what art may be allowed to do. We are forced to look beyond the limitations we ordinarily impose on art as an imitation of life, to look at the transparencies of the artifice as legitimate containers for meaning that cannot finally be reduced to the forms of expressive art.[11]

Some of those who celebrate the "serenity" of the plays also suggest a certain carelessness or indifference on Shakespeare's part about the making of the play. Morton Luce, for example, states: "In these later plays . . . their author writes, if not carelessly, at least with less of concentrated artistic determination and purpose; the evolution of a drama has become more of a recreation, less a matter of business. . . . the looking down from an Olympian height on mortal affairs, is less frequent and less distinct than the growing indifference to his dramatic business." [12] Both these celebrators and denigrators of the plays have one thing in common: they evaluate the stress on artifice as a relaxation on Shakespeare's part in the techniques of play-making. And most of these critics attempt to infer something about Shakespeare's frame

---

[11] Cf. Peter Ure's comment that "energy and meaning in the theatre may spring from the attempt to embody in its forms the very resistance which life offers to being translated into the expressive modes of art"; Ure, *Shakespeare: The Problem Plays* (London, 1961), 7.

[12] Morton Luce, Arden edition, *The Tempest* (London, 1926), lv–lvi. See Edwards, "Shakespeare's Romances," 2–3, for a discussion of other views of Shakespeare "on the heights."

of mind or spiritual attitude from what they consider to be a slackening of artistic control. There are obvious perils in this sort of evaluative transference, and they are finally unnecessary. To view the techniques of these late plays as consciously artificial for an artistic purpose is a more valuable way of discovering what these plays are really about, and it avoids limiting the scope of Shakespeare's achievement because of individual taste.

The heavy emphasis on artifice seems to be directed toward an affirmation of the rich potentialities which typically remain unrealized in everyday experiences. Simplifications and reductions to formula are instruments through which Shakespeare explores the distance between the potential and the actual, and between the yearning and the having. Rather than use the complexities bluntly as a means to define themselves, he focuses on the complexities through the simplicities which represent them. The word, the standard-bearer of thought and emotion, is ultimately less than that which it attempts to express. The dramatic logic involved in these last plays seems based on the recognition that methods of representation are inadequate for values they attempt to represent. This is why the audience is always being asked to look at the word, at the symbol, at the artifice, so that we can see how limited each reduction is. Expression of the fullness and the wonder of life is possible as the recognition occurs that the fullness and wonder are beyond man's powers of expression. In each of these four plays we are led, if we allow it, to accept the poetic lie as truth. The fairy tale proves to be a pattern of actual experience. Hermione lives in *The Winter's Tale*, and Leontes may very well question the manipulation of events that allows her to return to him (V.iii.139). But the return is so wonderful, so much better than man can afford to desire, that a little deception is not a difficult price to pay for the experience—especially when the audience has been told all along it is being deceived.

In his survey of the criticism of the last plays for the years 1900–57, Philip Edwards suggests that the line of investigation needed is one which asks, "What kind of emotional response were the Romances designed to arouse?" [13] Efforts have been made since 1957 to meet this need, and these works, among which I would categorize my study, might be classified as rhetorical approaches to the last plays. This approach primarily attempts to discern the mode of the plays by defining how the audience is led to respond to them in predictable ways. A brief survey of other critical approaches to these plays will indicate how the rhetorical approach overlaps and differs from others.[14]

Morton Luce and Lytton Strachey in their opposite views represent the biographical approach: the plays are assumed to reflect how Shakespeare himself felt at the time he wrote them. A more subtle, but similar, approach is the one which attempts to describe the canon as an organic development, leading (somehow inevitably) from one attitude to another and finally resulting in a vision that subsumes and transcends all of Shakespeare's preceding views of life. For example, E. M. W. Tillyard suggests that the last plays complete the tragic pattern begun in earlier plays.[15] G. Wilson Knight finds that *Henry VIII* is a more "satisfying" conclusion to Shakespeare's canon than *The Tempest* because it expresses

[13] Edwards, "Shakespeare's Romances," 17.

[14] I am indebted to Edwards' survey for the organization of the following discussion. Other important surveys of criticism on the last plays appear in the introduction to each play in the Arden edition. F. R. Leavis' caveat on "The Criticism of Shakespeare's Late Plays" appears in *The Common Pursuit* (New York, 1952), 173–81.

[15] E. M. W. Tillyard, *Shakespeare's Last Plays* (London, 1938), 16–22.

"a less visionary and enigmatic conclusion." [16] Knight's choice for Shakespeare's "crowning work" depends upon his own nationalistic vision; and it points up the primary error in viewing the canon as developing a specific pattern. One need only rearrange the order of the plays after 1603 to see how far the desire for symmetry may be a misleading factor in evaluating the last plays. [17] The idea that the "final" plays appropriately conclude the artistic life of the greatest English playwright because they are serene or mystic (or perhaps because they are incapable of being defined at all) is a tempting but potentially misleading angle of vision.

More objective is the approach expressed by G. E. Bentley in *Shakespeare and His Theatre*. [18] Bentley fails to consider *Pericles* as part of the group because it was written and performed before the Blackfriars theater was leased to the King's Men. [19] *Pericles*, however, clearly shares the dominant characteristics of the other three plays, and its earlier dating suggests that Shakespeare's dramaturgical explorations in this different genre were coincident with, but not dependent upon, acquiring a different theater for the performance of his plays. The external requirements of the theater itself thus need to be considered in conjunction with other dramatic materials which Shakespeare had at hand. E. C. Pettet attempts to formulate the characteristics of the romance tradition in which the last plays participate. [20] For him, the

[16] Knight, *The Crown of Life*, 256.

[17] Barroll's evidence in "The Chronology of Shakespeare's Jacobean Plays," suggests that several "accepted" datings of the plays may need revision.

[18] G. E. Bentley, *Shakespeare and His Theatre* (Lincoln, Nebr., 1964), 65–99.

[19] See Edwards' discussion of the omissions in Bentley's argument, "Shakespeare's Romances," 5.

[20] E. C. Pettet, *Shakespeare and the Romance Tradition* (London, 1949), 162–99.

chief characteristic of romance is a good story filled with incident and removed from considerations of verisimilitude. Shakespeare's earlier comedies use some of the same romance conventions that the last plays do, but the later "romances" differ from the comedies in their looser plot structure, their less convincing motivation, their concern with evil, and their emphasis on reconciliation through penitence and forgiveness. Pettet considers also the different kind of love-interest which revolves about older lovers and married love, the "decrease of the comic element," [21] and the change in poetic style.

A certain uneasiness arises from viewing the plays in terms of the romance tradition alone, because the strictures of classification occasionally impose limits on what Shakespeare was free to do with the romance conventions. This unnecessary limitation becomes clear in Pettet's and in J. M. Nosworthy's observations on characterization. Pettet says that the characters are puppets and that their emotions are spurious; Nosworthy insists that they "should be."

> The characters in *Cymbeline* are similarly disproportionate. In overweighting the action Shakespeare also overweights the agents and there is, at times, a destructive reality about the main personages of the play. Conventional romance makes little use of characterization. . . . Since Posthumus, who is quite one of the dullest of Shakespeare's heroes, never really comes to life, it should not be difficult for him to sustain this role of perfect knighthood, and we should never call his honour and virtue into question. But we do. . . . The romantic heroine should be the very perfection of beauty and virtue, the idealized, ethereal, passive princess of fairy-tale, divorced from the trivialities of everyday

[21] *Ibid.*, 186. This is a questionable assertion, I think. On the distinctions between the earlier comedies and the last plays, see Hoeniger's introduction to *Pericles*, Arden edition, lxxii–lxxiii.

life. . . . In Imogen, the conception is impaired by excessive vitality.[22]

Clearly, too great an insistence on Shakespeare's observance of an established tradition imposes unnecessary limitations on his art. It is important and necessary to delineate the traditions out of which these plays grew, but it is rash to insist that Shakespeare should have limited himself to any given pattern. To suggest, as Nosworthy does, that *Cymbeline* fails because Shakespeare did not transfer the "puppet characters" of narrative romance into drama is to neglect the possibility that Shakespeare did not aim at such a limited goal.[23]

Besides the chivalric romance conventions, the medieval tradition of exemplary romance and miracle play also appears to have influenced the last plays. F. D. Hoeniger suggests that *Pericles* is modeled after the saint's play and that the whole is constructed "to serve an explicit didactic end." [24] Because the protagonist of *Pericles* commits no sin, Robert G. Hunter excludes it from his consideration of the "problem plays" and "romances" which have in common a denouement of forgiveness.[25] Nonetheless, his study resembles Hoeniger's in that Hunter examines the tradition of the medieval miracle play, which builds its crisis upon the didactic Christian doctrine of forgiveness, as a significant influence on the structure of the last plays. L. G. Salingar likewise concentrates on the tradition (both classical and medieval) of exemplary romance to show how Shakespeare

[22] Nosworthy, introduction to the Arden edition of *Cymbeline*, lii, lx, lxi.

[23] See J. F. Danby, *Poets on Fortune's Hill* (London, 1952), 87–107; and Frank Kermode's introduction to *The Tempest*, Arden edition, for further discussions of the influence of the romance tradition on these plays.

[24] Hoeniger, introduction to the Arden edition of *Pericles*, lxxxviii.

[25] Robert G. Hunter, *Shakespeare and the Comedy of Forgiveness* (New York and London, 1965), 140–41.

seemed "to be aiming at a synthesis of Renaissance and medieval methods of stagecraft." [26]

Another tradition which influenced the shape of the last plays, but which is sometimes dismissed because of its vagueness, is tragicomedy. Native English tradition favored a mixture of kinds in drama;[27] and the theoretic articulation of tragicomedy from Italy joined with native inclination to influence the development of tragicomedy into a recognized mode in English practice. The foremost critical voice in the development of a Renaissance theory of tragicomedy was Giambattista Guarini.[28] He was the first to consider the term *tragicomedy* as a serious title for a genre distinct from either tragedy or comedy, and his *Il compendio della poesia tragicomica* (1601), written in defense of his play *Il Pastor Fido*, seems to have encouraged Renaissance playwrights to experiment in the genre.[29] Guarini praises tragicomedy as a higher form than either tragedy or comedy because the mixed genre "does not allow hearers to fall into excessive tragic melancholy or comic relaxation." [30] Guarini's concern with the effect on the audience is evident throughout his discussion of formal theory, but it is especially clear in his

[26] L. G. Salingar, "Time and Art in Shakespeare's Romances," *Renaissance Drama*, IX (1966), 24.

[27] In *The Defense of Poesie*, Sir Philip Sidney comments favorably on the practice of mingling kinds in poetry, although he also criticizes the writing of "mongrel tragicomedy." For appropriate passages, see Allan H. Gilbert, *Literary Criticism: Plato to Dryden* (New York, 1940), 430, sec. 29, and 451, sec. 49.

[28] For discussion of Guarini's influence, see Frank H. Ristine, *English Tragicomedy* (New York, 1910), 33–41; Eugene M. Waith, *The Pattern of Tragicomedy in Beaumont and Fletcher* (New Haven, 1952), 46–50; Madeline Doran, *Endeavors of Art* (Madison, Wis., 1964), 203–209; and Marvin T. Herrick, *Tragicomedy* (Urbana, Ill., 1962), 130–42.

[29] See Waith, *Pattern of Tragicomedy*, 45–47, for a discussion of Ben Jonson's interest in the genre and for the iconographical representation of tragicomedy which appears on the title page of the 1616 Folio of Jonson's *Workes*.

[30] Quoted in Gilbert, *Literary Criticism*, 512, sec. 136.

definition of tragicomic purpose—"to purge the mind from the evil affection of melancholy." [31] The tragicomic catharsis draws its strength from modifying and mingling tragic and comic methods and "pleasures." From tragedy, the author of tragicomedy takes "great persons but not great action; a plot which is verisimilar but not true; passions, moved but tempered; the delight, not the sadness; the danger, not the death; from the other [comedy], laughter which is not dissolute, modest amusement, a feigned complication, a happy reversal, and above all, the comic order." [32]

John Fletcher's definition of tragicomedy in his Preface to the First Quarto of *The Faithful Shepherdess* (c. 1608–10) echoes Guarini's formal theory as well as his defensive position: "A tragi-comedy is not so called in respect of mirth and killing, but in respect it wants deaths, which is enough to make it no tragedy, yet brings some near it, which is enough to make it no comedy, which must be a representation of familiar people, with such kind of trouble as no life be questioned; so that a god is as lawful in this as in a tragedy, and mean people as in a comedy." [33] Fletcher's definition, like Guarini's, concentrates on the social position of its characters and on the ending—conventional concerns of formal theorists about tragedy and comedy. Fletcher's definition is a great simplification of Guarini's vision of tragicomic purpose, but derivative categories suggest that Guarini's arguments had been listened to in England. The most resounding evidence that awareness of tragicomedy as a legitimate genre was increasing is the number of plays written and produced in the seventeenth century that either fall into

[31] *Ibid.*, 522, sec. 22b.

[32] This is Waith's translation of Guarini. Waith, *Pattern of Tragicomedy*, 48.

[33] Francis Beaumont and John Fletcher, *The Works of Beaumont and Fletcher*, ed. Alexander Dyce (11 vols.; London, 1843), II, 17.

that classification or that verge upon it.[34] Tragicomedy, because of its assimilative nature, has never had an absolute definition and seems to have been open to variations according to the playwright's predispositions. Shakespeare's work in the genre differs from that of other dramatists; but one of the characteristics that his tragicomedies share with others is a great stress on artifice.

Several critics have formulated theories about the purpose of this emphasis on artifice in Shakespeare's last plays. S. L. Bethell suggests that the antiquated techniques and other artifices liberate *The Winter's Tale* from one kind of reality in order to express another.[35] Nevill Coghill argues that devices such as the bear, Father Time, and the statue's coming to life are not crude techniques but highly sophisticated stagecraft.[36] Bethell and Coghill agree that Shakespeare makes the audience aware of the devices. As Bethell suggests, they recognize that the devices are in themselves comically inadequate expressions of life. But also, as Coghill insists, these devices control the audience's responses in complex and subtle ways and are therefore "new" and sophisticated techniques. Maynard Mack has an important essay on Shakespeare's use of audience "engagement and detachment," but he glances only briefly at three examples in the last plays.[37] Mack says that the "most vexing problem of the Elizabethan acting

---

[34] See Ristine's list of almost 250 English tragicomedies in the appendix, *English Tragicomedy*, 207–28.

[35] S. L. Bethell, *The Winter's Tale: A Study* (London, 1947), 47–48.

[36] Nevill Coghill, "Six Points of Stage-Craft in *The Winter's Tale*," *Shakespeare Survey*, XI (1958), 31–42.

[37] Maynard Mack, "Engagement and Detachment in Shakespeare's Plays," in Richard Hosley (ed.), *Essays on Shakespeare and Elizabethan Drama in Honor of Hardin Craig* (Columbia, Mo., 1962), 275–96. Other essays which consider in some detail the effects of self-conscious artistry and the principle of engagement and detachment, and which draw conclusions similar to my own, are Barbara A. Mowat, "*Cymbeline*: Crude Dramaturgy and Aesthetic Distance," in George Walton Williams (ed.),

company's art" was "how to mime reality in its grander forms without riveting attention on the inadequacy of the means." [38] In the last plays (as well as in some earlier ones), Shakespeare seems to have purposefully directed attention to the inadequacy of the means, which suggests that he was experimenting with the problem as well as with the methods for handling it. Bertrand Evans, in a more limiting but similar attempt to define the uses of audience awareness, concludes that the last plays are peculiarly full of exploited discrepancies between the awarenesses of the audience and of the participants in the plays. Of the deceit involved in Hermione's return to life in *The Winter's Tale*, Evans says, "this is very shrewd dramatic practice—like eating one's cake and having it too, but even more like eating it two or three times and having it too." [39] The awareness of being on the inside and on the outside of the play simultaneously is not peculiar to the last plays, but the emphasis on contradictory awarenesses held at the same time comes under greater stress in the tragicomedies.

Granville-Barker's evaluation of this double awareness makes two important points: first, the intentional use of self-conscious theatrics creates a tragicomic perspective; and second, the audience feels a sense of power by being allowed to share the playwright's control of the action.

> This art, which deliberately displays its art, is very suited to a tragi-comedy, to the telling of a serious story that must yet not be taken too seriously, lest its comedy be swamped by its tragedy and a happy ending become too incongruous. ... The emphasizing of the artifice, the 'folly of the fiction,'

Renaissance Papers, 1966 (Durham, N.C., 1967), 39–47; Arthur C. Kirsch, "*Cymbeline* and Coterie Dramaturgy," *ELH*, XXXIV (1967), 285–306; and William H. Matchett, "Some Dramatic Techniques in 'The Winter's Tale'," *Shakespeare Survey*, XXII (1969), 93–107.

[38] Mack, "Engagement and Detachment," 284.
[39] Evans, *Shakespeare's Comedies*, 315.

by which Cloten's corpse comes to be mistaken for Post-humus' does much to mitigate the crude horror of the business, to bring it into the right tragi-comic key. Keep us intrigued by the preparations for the trick, and we shall gain from its accomplishment a half-professional pleasure; we shall be masters of the illusion, not its victims. And throughout the whole elaborate scene of revelation with which the play ends we are most artfully steered between illusion and enjoyment of the ingenuity of the thing.[40]

The perspective of this mixed mode insists on a balance between comedy and tragedy at all times. This balance depends upon a fusion of the two modes rather than upon mere alternation or juxtaposition of them, a point upon which Guarini insists: "For he who makes a tragicomedy does not intend to compose separately either a tragedy or a comedy, but from the two a third thing that will be perfect of its kind." [41] As Granville-Barker says, the balance of tragedy and comedy is achieved partially through the distance that self-conscious use of theatrical device gains. Theatrical signs are not always used simply to keep the stark effects of an action from gaining too much of an emotional response from the audience, as in the instance of Cloten's beheading, or as in the case of Antigonus' being devoured by a bear in *The Winter's Tale*. In fact, even these examples have a much more complex dramatic value than this achievement of distance. However, emotional distance is one significant result of having the theatricality of the action emphasized to such a degree that it must be recognized. The audience cannot remain under a spell, perceiving an illusion as actual, when it is forced to recognize that the thing itself is patently illusory. They are involved in the action at the same time they are forced to look at it from a distance. The first kind of response promotes a feeling that pertinent issues are under vital consid-

[40] Granville-Barker, *Prefaces to Shakespeare*, II, 244–47.
[41] Quoted in Gilbert, *Literary Criticism*, 507.

eration; and the second leads to a critical evaluation of what those issues can mean in a world outside the playhouse. The process of calling attention to the artifice thus requires a double commitment from the audience. At first the involvement in the illusion is noncritical; disbelief is suspended. But then the artifice forces an examination of the difference between this illusion and the actual. The audience then recommits itself to the illusion, but now with the sense of the actual behind the affirmation of the illusory. As Mack says, "the total moral weight of comedy inclines generally toward the detached man, as that of tragedy inclines toward the man engaged."[42] Although Mack is speaking of the characterization of the protagonist, his distinction applies equally well to the response of the audience. In comedy, the distance of the audience from the characters' plights is central to the effect; in tragedy, the closeness of the audience to the characters' crises is an ultimate factor in the achievement of its catharsis. In Shakespeare's tragicomedies, however, there is a simultaneous emphasis on both engagement and detachment producing a state of wonderment which holds these apparently opposite responses in equilibrium.

Granville-Barker's second point is that the playwright grants manipulative power to the audience, or at least seems to grant it. He suggests that when the playwright allows us to see the preparations of a trick, we then become half-professional partners in watching the trick's accomplishment: we are "masters of the illusion, not its victim." In *The Winter's Tale*, of course, Shakespeare hides from his audience the fact that Hermione remains alive and we are thus the victims, rather than the masters of this illusion. Even in this play, however, the audience is prepared just in advance of the characters to know that Hermione still lives. In

---

[42] Mack, "Engagement and Detachment," 287.

the other plays the audience consistently knows much more than the characters and feels like a participant in creating the staged illusion. This is most true of *The Tempest*, when Prospero announces in his Epilogue that the audience has the power to confine him on his bare isle or to send him to Naples. This sense of kinship with the playwright, although conventional in epilogues, is stressed to an extraordinary degree in Prospero's parting speech; and this speech typifies an important aspect of the tragicomic vision which Shakespeare creates. The audience seems to watch on the same level as the playwright while the illusion becomes actual.

The implications of the audience's being master of the illusion are more far-reaching than Granville-Barker suggests, however. In these last plays, the world of man's actions and the world of divine control come together in "rare visions" of reality. Man discovers that his motives and actions do not produce unalterable consequences, even when they seem to do so. The effect of any human cause may be transformed into a different effect by an agency more powerful than man. There is reassurance in this recognition. In *Othello*, Desdemona dies as a result of Othello's jealousy; but in *The Winter's Tale*, Hermione lives or, more precisely, returns to life despite the destructive jealousy of Leontes. Man's actions do not produce irrecoverable effects in the tragicomedies; in fact, the accepted relationship between cause and consequence dissolves. The knowledge that apparently unleashable forces are being controlled by a benevolent power allows us to entertain threats of evil because we are assured that they will ultimately be thwarted. We can safely invest our emotions in a world where evil only seems to be in control.[43]

The affirmation of divine control is a signal characteristic

[43] Cf. Theodore Spencer, "Appearance and Reality in Shakespeare's Last Plays," *Modern Philology*, XXXIX (1942), 269.

of Shakespeare's tragicomedies. Of course, many of Shakespeare's plays affirm such authority. Two distinctions characterize the tragicomedies, however: the way in which the supernatural figures are brought onstage,[44] and the way in which the audience is drawn into action that repeats divine action. By establishing a kinship between the playwright and the audience as controllers of the illusion, Shakespeare forces his audience to know, through experience, the obligations as well as the privileges of authority. When Prospero pleads for "indulgence" from his audience in the Epilogue, he is insisting that they recognize the analogue between human and divine action.

> As you from crimes would pardon'd be,
> Let your indulgence set me free.

This is not simply an appeal for a balanced return of indulgence for indulgence; it is an invitation to see the analogous relationship between man's capacity to forgive and divine grace. As the audience is to Prospero, so Prospero has been to the other characters of the play in choosing virtue over vengeance. And, most significantly, as Prospero acts toward men in the play, so Providence acts toward humanity. Forgiveness is no longer a mere abstraction; it has been vitalized through the artifice of the theater; Prospero's plea is ostensibly for the indulgence of applause, but behind that surface lies a greater claim. Drama is an imitation of life in more than the action represented on the stage. The theatrical fiction becomes a metaphor through which larger issues may be comprehended. Fantasy is the means by which the audience

[44] The difference in the handling of supernatural figures can be seen most readily in the descent of Diana in *Pericles* (V.i) and of Jupiter in *Cymbeline* (V.iv). Apollo is presented more obliquely through his oracle in *The Winter's Tale*, and Prospero integrates the descent of the god with his human nature in *The Tempest*. In all four cases, the inclusion of the controlling deity on the level of man's actions unabashedly disregards a "realistic" explanation through cause and effect.

is led to understand the truth about the actual lives they live.

I am not convinced by Anne Righter's assertions about *The Tempest* that "reality in this domain of the play dissolves and is lost in a confusion of dreams and shadows" and that "the condition of the actor and the man who watches his performance in the theatre have become identical." [45] There is an unquestionable blurring of the distinctions between stage illusion and actual experience, as Mrs. Righter demonstrates, but she focuses too exclusively on Prospero's speech at the end of the wedding masque in Act IV. This speech is, after all, not the final action of the play, nor does it control the final effect. The reunion of the play's characters follows this speech and the Epilogue reinstates the stage metaphor. I agree that the process of drawing the audience into the illusion causes a dislocation of perspective so that "resemblance" does for a time fuse into "identity." But the ultimate effect of the play is to resolve this dislocation through a new perspective which again distinguishes between the theater and life so that the audience sees itself in an analogous, rather than in an identical, position with the players. The consciousness of artifice accomplishes this recognition. If the divergence of these two realms did not occur, the didactic effect of the play would be lessened. The important impact at the end of each of these tragicomedies is the audience's renewed awareness of art as a focusing agent for reality. If actuality and illusion were inseparable at the conclusion, as Mrs. Righter states, the final effect would be as she suggests: "Life has been engulfed by illusion." This is, in fact, the penultimate stage of the tragicomic process. The ultimate resolution depends upon it but does not remain in

[45] Anne Righter, *Shakespeare and the Idea of the Play* (London, 1964), 201–204. Mrs. Righter uses *The Tempest* as the culminative example of the techniques used in the three other plays. I have also assumed that *The Tempest* is representative in this way.

it. The end of the play renews the distinction between the audience and the players, so that their similarities may be understood and evaluated. The world of the actual has been illuminated through the illusion, but the audience is nonetheless aware of the difference.

As an example of this process of fusion and reemergence, consider the last act of *Pericles*. When the hero is on the brink of knowing that the girl standing before him is his daughter, whom he had supposed dead, he asks her to pause in the process of her revelation.

> O, stop there a little!
> This is the rarest dream that e'er dull'd sleep
> Did mock sad fools withal; this cannot be
> My daughter, buried.
>
> (V.i.160–64)

Having just been revived from an emotional death, from his spiritual isolation, Pericles wants to savor this moment when the impossible world of dreams and the actual world of experience are about to coalesce. The hesitation, the desire to delay the revelation which will drive two worlds into a union from which they will again diverge, is a delicate and comic desire. It is delicate because it wishes to preserve that essential perfection which the culmination of action can achieve; it is comic because change is the ultimate operative in the process of human life, even in the world of Shakespeare's final plays. The balance achieved in Pericles' expression of his wish to preserve this exquisite motion toward recognition is common to each of these last four plays, and, in each case, it depends upon the knowledge that man is moving. In this particular speech, the balance is between a world which has denied Pericles all rewards, all joys, and a world which grants him all he has previously desired. His hesitation in accepting the world which fulfills his wishes, his savoring of the moment penultimate to resolution, credits both the former and the future worlds with meaning. Such moments of delicate balance on the verge of worlds which are fusing become the rare visions out of which these final plays are made.

From this fusion of worlds, however, the play moves forward through theatrically contrived artifice to a reassertion of the distinction between the world of the theater and the world of the audience. Diana descends and directs Pericles to her temple at Ephesus; Gower intervenes with a narrative "bridge"; and the recovery of Thaisa is enacted before a tableaulike assemblage at Diana's temple. The last scene includes such stylized actions as the recognition of love tokens, Thaisa's joyful swoon, renewed vows of love and fidelity, and praise of Diana and the gods for their mercy. Then, with the Epilogue, Gower returns to review and complete the various lines of action and to wish the audience "joy."

> So on your patience evermore attending,
> New joy wait on you! Here our play has ending.

Only two points need concern us here: the audience, first, is made very much aware of theatrical contrivances and, second, is invited to view its own position as analogous to that of the players. The play now ends, but the audience's lives continue. New joy has come to the players; Gower wishes that similar blessings may await the audience. As Gower points out in his Prologue, his story is an old one, "And lords and ladies in their lives / Have read it for restoratives." The play is not only about restoration; it provides the means of restoring the audience itself. The "evil affection of melancholy" has been purged.

Neither *Cymbeline* nor *The Winter's Tale* has an epilogue; thus, there is no explicit invitation to the audience to view itself from an analogous position. Nonetheless, there is heavy emphasis on conscious artifice in the final scenes of both plays. *Cymbeline*'s recognition and recovery scene brings together so many lines of plot that it is no small feat to list all of them. Reconciliations are effected between Posthumus and Imogen, Cymbeline and Imogen, Cymbeline and Belarius, Cymbeline and his two lost sons, Iachimo and those he has injured, and between England and Rome, to name the major ones. The very skillfulness with which all this complexity of matter is handled calls attention to itself. The exaggerated complexity is bewildering to the players as well as to the audience. Cymbeline comments from time to time on the excess of revelation:

> Is there more? . . .
> New matter still. . . .
> When shall I hear all through?
> (V.v.48, 243, 383)

Cymbeline voices what any audience to these complexly interwoven revelations must feel, and because he recognizes the excess, he mitigates the sense of implausibility to some degree. He is very much aware of his position as an audience without an active part to play, and he is somewhat chagrined by his passivity. He insists that Imogen allow him a role in her drama of revelations.

> How now, my flesh, my child?
> What, mak'st thou me a dullard in this act?
> Wilt thou not speak to me?
> (V.v.264–66)

The consciousness of theatricality is common to the other players, too, and the audience can hardly miss the pointed references to it. This emphasis on artifice brings the focus into the heart of the matter: How does art relate to life? Art and life seem to be inextricably intertwined through a kind of magic completion—each seems to reflect and fulfill the other.

Leontes becomes aware of this in the statue scene which closes *The Winter's Tale*. Thinking the statue to be only a statue, Leontes is overwhelmed by the exactitude with which art has imitated life:

> Leon. The fixure of her eye has motion in 't,
> As we are mock'd with art.
> Paul.   I'll draw the curtain:
> My lord's almost so far transported that
> He'll think anon it lives.
> Leon.   O sweet Paulina,
> Make me to think so twenty years together!
> No settled senses of the world can match
> The pleasure of that madness. Let 't alone.
> (V.iii.67–73)

Art, in this instance, seems more vital than life, more real. Life is "mock'd" both in the sense that art imitates life and in the sense that art points out life's limitations.[46] Art has given Hermione a vitality which she did not have before. When Leontes sees the statue of Hermione, he sees her as she is (even to her wrinkles) not as he had previously created her in his mad dream of evil. The statue renews Leontes' vision; and his perception of the statue, the true Hermione, allows her to return to life. The plays, similarly, give life to the imagination of their audience even as they are given life by it.

This imaginative renewal depends upon the audience's recognition of artifice as artificial, and it is unfortunate that so often readers and spectators respond to this recognition

[46] Pericles likewise uses the word "mock'd" when he begins to perceive that Marina is his daughter: V.i.141–43, 161–62.

with embarrassment.[47] This reaction is due, no doubt, to a dubious sense of sophistication that has come to be associated with realism or naturalism as the most meaningful expressive mode in literature. There is sometimes a tendency to think that the difference between art and life is best when minimized, and that the increase of distance between them leans toward escapism. This is perhaps a shaky assumption; but, even with it, many critics have pointed out that the art of Shakespeare's last plays cannot fairly be considered as escapist art because there are too many reminders that life is a treacherous business.[48]

The pressure of the actual on the remote is one of the chief distinguishing characteristics of Shakespeare's tragicomedies. Other writers of tragicomedy make use of a counterbalance between the familiar and the remote,[49] but Shakespeare's handling of it marks his plays with a difference. The final vision of his tragicomedies is a reunion of the realm of human action and the realm of the divine. Beaumont and Fletcher, the most important contemporary practitioners of the mode, direct the balance of the remote and familiar toward a fuller realization of emotional response in their audience, but they tend to discard possibilities for exploiting meaningful analogies between the play's action and the lives of the audience.

For instance, in *A King and No King*, Arbaces graciously forgives his mother for her plot against his life. When the

[47] Consider, as an example, the response of a spectator after the Edinburgh Festival production of *The Winter's Tale* (1966): "Delightful, of course, but no one can think that Shakespeare was *serious* when he wrote it."

[48] See Hunter, *Shakespeare and the Comedy of Forgiveness*, 184, 202–203, 240–41; Evans, *Shakespeare's Comedies*, 220 ff.; Robert Ornstein, *The Moral Vision of Jacobean Tragedy* (Madison, Wis., 1960), 224–27; Patrick Cruttwell, *The Shakespearean Moment* (New York, 1960), 103; and D. R. C. Marsh, *The Recurring Miracle* (Lincoln, Nebr., 1969), 192–97.

[49] See Waith, *Pattern of Tragicomedy*, 36.

Queen-mother kneels, Arbaces dispenses with decorum in a touching display of human loyalty.

> *Arbaces.*   Oh, stand up
> And let me kneel; the light will be asham'd
> To see observance done to me by you.
> *Arane.*   You are my king.
> *Arbaces.*   You are my mother; rise.
> As far be all your faults from your own soul
> As from my memory; then you shall be
> As white as innocence herself.
>
> (III.i.47–53) [50]

Yet, in the next moment the note of the emotionally familiar gives place to the extravagance of Arbaces' refusal to recognize his sister's existence. Such a juxtaposition does not explore psychological truths that may lead to self-knowledge for Arbaces; it exists rather for the contrast of emotional responses in the audience which the narrative action may supplement but does not direct.[51] It turns out, of course, that the Queen-mother had tried to poison Arbaces for fear that her deception in naming him as her son would be discovered and she would be denounced as a traitor (V.iv.241–50), but the narrative pertinence of her motive does not affect Arbaces' forgiveness of her actions before he discovers the motive.

Consider, in contrast, the way in which the evil queen of fairy-tale convention is treated in *Cymbeline*. She also tries to poison the heir apparent, her stepdaughter Imogen, in order to place her son Cloten on the throne of England. Yet her motive is revealed early in the play by the physician Cornelius, who substitutes a sleeping potion for the poison

---

[50] Citations of *A King and No King* are from the Regents Renaissance Drama edition, edited by Robert K. Turner, Jr. (Lincoln, Nebr., 1963).

[51] See Arthur Mizener's discussion of the sequence, "The High Design of *A King and No King*," *Modern Philology*, XXXVIII (1940–41), 144–49; and Waith's analysis of the same scene, *Pattern of Tragicomedy*, 32–33.

she has requested (I.vi.33–44). Her deception, when it is revealed in the final scene, enlarges upon the problem of perceiving true virtue despite appearances around which the play's entire action centers. Appealing to familiar emotions, Cymbeline says:

> Mine eyes
> Were not in fault, for she was beautiful:
> Mine ears that heard her flattery, nor my heart
> That thought her like her seeming. It had been vicious
> To have mistrusted her: yet, O my daughter,
> That it was folly in me, thou mayst say,
> And prove it in thy feeling. Heaven mend all!
>
> (V.v.62–68)

To be deceived by beauty is a familiar experience, and the human touch does much to restore Cymbeline to the happy ending of the play: it counteracts his remoteness as a stereotyped tyrant in the earlier scenes of the play. Arbaces' familial loyalty to his ill-intentioned mother creates the same kind of counteraction, but the balance is not directed toward a moral frame of reference as it is in *Cymbeline*.

In achieving the tragicomic denouement also, Beaumont and Fletcher differ from Shakespeare. With the exception of *The Winter's Tale*, Shakespeare gives his audience the key to the miracle well ahead of the characters' discovery of it, and even in *The Winter's Tale* the audience receives clues to the turning of that key before Leontes and the others know what it is. Beaumont and Fletcher characteristically withhold the vital key until the final scene, so that the audience is surprised to the same degree as the characters in the play. In *Philaster*, the reversal of fortunes comes when the page Bellario reveals himself to be Euphrasia, the daughter of a Sicilian nobleman. The revelation clears the good name of Arethusa and effects the reinstatement of Philaster as rightful heir to the crown of Sicily. Similarly, in the last scene of *A King and No King,* Gobrius reveals that Arbaces is his son and not the brother of Panthea, for whom Arbaces has conceived a passionate love. The triple catastrophe of murder, incest, and suicide which Arbaces had threatened is thus averted and the "comic order" is restored.

In Shakespeare's last plays the denouement is likewise a happy reversal, but the audience knows what the agent of the reversal will be long before the characters know. In *Pericles,* for instance, immediately following Pericles' burial of Thaisa in the sea, we witness her recovery to life by Cerimon (III.ii). Cymbeline's daughter, Imogen, like Euphrasia in *Philaster,* has disguised herself as a page (III.iv); but Imogen dons her disguise before the eyes of the audience and we are prepared for the reversal which her revelation of that disguise makes possible in the final scene.[52] In *The Tempest,* Prospero informs us that "there's no harm done" (I.ii. 15) and that he has determined upon "virtue" rather than "vengeance" (V.i.28). As I have already suggested, Shakespeare's drawing of the audience into his confidence is a determining characteristic of his particular goals for tragicomedy. In this distinction between his plays and those of Beaumont and Fletcher lies an indication of the vast difference in the purpose each had in using the mode.

The "protean characters" are another of Fletcher's characteristics of tragicomedy, according to Waith's itemization. Marvin Herrick suggests that Beaumont and Fletcher were not unique in their sacrifice of consistent characterization and he cites Shakespeare's Posthumus and Leontes as proofs of his assertion.[53] As I hope to show in the chapter on *Cymbeline,* however, Posthumus is not an "unpredictable" char-

[52] Although many critics have considered *Philaster* to be a source for *Cymbeline,* Harold S. Wilson convincingly demonstrates major differences between these two plays in "*Philaster* and *Cymbeline,*" in Alan S. Downer (ed.), *English Institute Essays, 1951* (New York, 1952), 146–67.

[53] Herrick, *Tragicomedy,* 263.

acter. He develops according to naturalistic psychological criteria.[54] And Leontes too, after his apparently unmotivated jealousy in the first act, develops consistently.[55]

Perhaps the most significant way in which Shakespeare brings the pressure of the actual to bear upon the dramatic illusion, in contrast with the practice of Beaumont and Fletcher, is in the occurrence of deaths. Fletcher states in his Preface to *The Faithful Shepherdess* that tragicomedy "wants deaths . . . yet brings some near it," following Guarini's stricture. In Shakespeare's plays the chief characters do escape death, but, in each play except *The Tempest*, death occurs to secondary characters. In the cases of *Pericles* and *Cymbeline*, the deaths are a matter of poetic justice (except for Simonides, who dies naturally of old age). The wicked Antiochus and his daughter, as well as Cleon and Dionyza, are struck down by divine vengeance in *Pericles*, and both sets of deaths are only reported (by Helicanus, II.iv; and by Gower in his Epilogue). In *Cymbeline*, however, when Cloten's severed head is brought onstage (IV.ii), the fact of death disturbs the idyllic assumptions of the pastoral setting. Guiderius' casual dismissal of Cloten's head minimizes the seriousness of his death; just as the comic expansiveness of Cornelius' report in the final scene reduces the serious impact of the Queen's death. Nonetheless, the actual world invades the conventional world of romance more in Shakespeare's play than either Guarini or Fletcher allowed for. In

---

[54] This naturalness has been noticed by other critics, especially by Una Ellis-Fermor, *The Jacobean Drama* (London, 1958), 211 n. 1. Harold Wilson discusses the more "serious" character of Posthumus as compared to Philaster, "*Philaster* and *Cymbeline*," 161.

[55] Matchett, "Some Dramatic Techniques in 'The Winter's Tale'," 97, points out that Leontes has a great deal of motivation for his jealousy in the language that Hermione and Polixenes use in I.ii. He says, "Far from feeling that Leontes is too rapidly jealous, we should feel that he has been very slow about it." This slight exaggeration does help to balance the traditional view that Leontes' jealousy is inexplicable.

The Winter's Tale, the deaths are even more of an encroach-
ment of the actual upon the illusionary world of fairy tale.
It is possible to excuse them as poetic justice, insofar as Leontes must suffer real loss for his assumption of godhood, and
because Antigonus erred in believing Hermione guilty of
adultery and in abandoning her child on the coast of Bohemia. Yet Leontes' son Mamillius is innocent himself and
his death is a sacrifice made to alter the course of Leontes'
madness. The dramatic presentation of both these deaths in
The Winter's Tale subordinates their troubling implications
to other, more important values, but the disturbing factors
are not wholly exorcised. This fact supports the conclusion
that Shakespeare did not want to create a world that could
float free of actuality or escape from life's meaningful issues.
On the other hand, Beaumont and Fletcher seem to minimize
the "seriousness" of art's relationship to life.

Even in the use of the "fable" as a plot structure, Shakespeare seems to have shaped the convention into his final
vision of cosmic harmony. The choice of a fabulous plot
increases the expectation that actions are under a control
which operates beyond man's power. The revelation of that
control to both the characters of the plays and the audience
in a manner which endorses its reality is the goal toward
which Shakespeare's tragicomic action moves. The revelation occurs after settled perspectives, or ways of seeing, have
been dislocated and values have been refocused. A broader
view succeeds the narrow, settled way of seeing. His method
of accomplishing this enlarged and multiple perspective is
the creation of wonder, which is more complex than Beaumont and Fletcher's creation of surprise. We are caught in
amazement as we look through the artistic illusion, with its
patently theatrical devices, into a level of reality toward
which we have yearned without knowing it. The use of
fable creates an expectation of wondrous action, but the ulti-

mate wonder is that we can accept, in Shakespeare's plays, the poetic lie as truth. Beaumont and Fletcher want us to look at the artifice and admire its ingenuity; but Shakespeare wants us to look through the artifice to see why it is worth the effort.

In each of Shakespeare's last plays the "rarest dream," the tragicomic vision, evolves through the separation of the central characters from the values they had held to be significant. Their separation from the world of "settled senses" in which they thought they knew how to see and to understand forces them to recreate an order of life independent of given values. Man's narrow perspective, which has closed out the vision of cosmic harmony and focused instead on human machinations, is forced to grow into a perspective which includes complex views of an epic scope: the individual's life achieves meaning by finding its context in all humanity. The significant difference between the characters' positions at the opening of the play and at the close is that they have become aware of their own fallibility, of their limitations in sustaining human relationships, and of their capacity to endure. The pattern of Shakespeare's tragicomic action, in the simplest terms, is to dislocate settled perceptions through adversity and then to liberate perception through unexpected prosperity. The expanded perceptions of each character reveal a world that is no longer confined by his own limitations. He has confronted a world constituted upon "nothing," and from this "nothing" meaning grows.[56] The reduction is a necessary prelude, as it is in the tragedies, to the realization that correspondences do exist

[56] The juggling of what is real and what is illusion has its most teasing manifestation in scenes which present the struggle against "nothing," a struggle for meaning in a world which is somehow dislocated. Shakespeare's use of "nothing" recurs throughout the canon, but with various values. Perhaps the most significant and clearest example of the semantic struggle to establish a meaningful philosophy is in *King Lear* in two scenes

between appearance and reality and between divine and human action, and that the characters may confidently rely upon them. The experience belongs not only to the characters of the play; Shakespeare's tragicomic method makes his vision, in a uniquely personal way, the vision which the audience knows is its own.

---

which parallel each other: the opening debate between Lear and Cordelia (I.i.87 ff.) and the later banter between Lear and his Fool (I.iv.134 ff.). Leontes has a tormented speech in *The Winter's Tale* in which he tries to convince Camillo (and himself as well) that he has not misconstrued his wife's actions (I.ii.284–96). In the last plays, the reduction to "nothing" is associated with the destruction of former attitudes and precedes the rebuilding of new and worthier attitudes. Also see Paul A. Jorgensen, "Much Ado About *Nothing*," *Shakespeare Quarterly*, V (1954), 287–95; Sigurd Burckhardt, "*King Lear*: The Quality of Nothing," *Minnesota Review*, II (1961), 33–50; Robert F. Fleissner, "The 'Nothing' Element in *King Lear*," *Shakespeare Quarterly*, XIII (1962), 67–70; Rosalie L. Colie, *Paradoxia Epidemica* (Princeton, 1966), 470–81; and G. Wilson Knight's note on the various uses of "nothing" in the plays, *The Crown of Life*, 82 n. 1.

Chapter II ✚ *PERICLES*
The Old
and the New

One of the features of *Pericles* that sets it apart from all other Shakespeare plays is the appearance of Gower, the poet who has been resurrected in order to present the play. As a "presenter" Gower resembles the Chorus in *Henry V*, but he is a historic personage rather than an anonymous one, like the Chorus, or an allegorical one, like "Rumour" in *2 Henry IV* or "Time" in *The Winter's Tale*.[1] Gower's reincarnation gives the initial impulse to the play's theme of loss and restoration; in addition, his presence as an "ancient" poet stresses the archaic qualities of both the "old song" and the old style in which it is to be sung.

> To sing a song that old was sung,
> From ashes ancient Gower is come,
> Assuming man's infirmities,
> To glad your ear, and please your eyes.
> It hath been sung at festivals,
> On ember-eves and holy-ales;
> And lords and ladies in their lives
> Have read it for restoratives:
> The purchase is to make men glorious,

[1] F. D. Hoeniger's introduction to the Arden edition of *Pericles* (London, 1963), xix–xxiii, lxxvi–lxxviii, contains an important discussion of Gower.

34

Et bonum quo antiquius eo melius.
If you, born in these latter times,
When wit's more ripe, accept my rimes,
And that to hear an old man sing
May to your wishes pleasure bring,
I life would wish, and that I might
Waste it for you like taper-light.

(Prol., 1–16)

The dedication of the playwright to the audience's pleasure is a conventional compliment that Shakespeare regularly made explicit in his comedies. But here, Gower's wish to renew life only to entertain the audience exaggerates a convention itself born of courteous hyperbole.

Gower's self-conscious emphasis on artificiality in his Prologue calls attention to several things. He states the "argument" for the play in conventionally epic terms, as Homer and Virgil had done before him. The echo places the play in the epic tradition and alerts the audience to anticipate a story of grand scope. Furthermore, his story has been "sung" and "read" repeatedly; its current revival links the art of the past with that of the present. The function of this art has been "restorative" and this, the audience can assume, is also its present purpose. Precisely what is to be restored remains for the play to define, but the relationship of art to life is clearly a salutary one. Gower's reincarnation "from ashes" presents one kind of restoration, and it creates an expectation for other kinds to follow: Pericles restores Tharsus by bringing corn for its famine; Cerimon revives Thaisa at Ephesus; Marina heals the moral decay of Mytilene and the emotional apathy of her father; and the members of Pericles' family are reunited. Each restoration is related to the previous ones and the repetition forms a pattern which helps to unify the play's action. The final restoration, as Gower suggests in his Epilogue, affects the audience itself. They must return to a life that differs from the theater's illusion, but they take with them renewed capacities for experiencing joy.

All of Gower's appearances have a double effect: on the most obvious level he is an extradramatic device used to integrate the narrative; but on a more subtle level, he visually realizes the idea that art's vitality can defeat the transience of life and death. He is both an artifice and the representation of art's perdurability. As such, he has extraordinary powers to condition the audience's response to the play. The old song that Gower sings is the story of a man buffeted by apparently adverse seas who discovers that the tempest is a prelude to rare serenity. The old style of Gower's narrative is a collection of archaic forms that exhibits the evolution of old art into new. Gower himself, singing his "rimes" to an audience born two centuries after his death, exemplifies how new art reanimates the old. The dumb show demonstrates the principle in another way.

Pericles contains three dumb shows, and the first two depict nothing more dramatic than the reading of a letter from Helicanus. All three of the dumb shows occur at a point when Pericles' course is again directed to the sea: in the first he has just relieved the people of Tharsus from famine, in the second he has comfortably settled with Thaisa in Pentapolis, and in the third he has returned to Tharsus to retrieve his daughter from Cleon and Dionyza. The pantomimes successfully link the large segments of dramatized action; and the repetition of this distinct presentational device provides a visual symmetry that makes the play's parts seem more coherent.[2] The dumb show's integration into the line of dramatic action refines the older uses of the device. In its earlier forms, the dumb show was often used as a diversion between acts, and it was accompanied by a presenter whose function

[2] See Dieter Mehl, *The Elizabethan Dumb Show: The History of a Dramatic Convention* (London, 1965), 158.

was to explain the pantomime's point. In the development of English drama, the dumb show became more closely interwoven into the dramatic action and the figure of the presenter underwent a similar integration. In the play scene of *Hamlet* (III.ii), perhaps the most brilliant use of the dumb show in English drama, Hamlet himself is in the position of presenter for the pantomime, even though he does not supply explicit summary of its meaning. The weaving of this antique form into the fabric of the play is more sophisticated in *Hamlet* than in *Pericles*, and the very lack of integration between Gower and the play he describes stresses the obvious artificiality of the device.

Gower's explanation of all the dumb shows in *Pericles* is so extensive that one wonders why the first two are necessary. Since the letters' contents are explained anyway, the visual elaboration seems excessive. Ostensibly they present little more than the reading of a letter, which hardly merits the attention of this special dramatic form. For example, Simonides enters reading a letter in II.iv, the content of which he makes known in a soliloquy (15 ff.). The pantomime, on the other hand, removes the scene from the realistic level and insists on its symbolic potentials. The stage directions suggest the quality of ritual.

> *Enter, at one door*, Pericles, *talking with* Cleon; *all the train with them. Enter, at another door, a Gentleman, with a letter to* Pericles; Pericles *shows the letter to* Cleon; Pericles *gives the Messenger a reward, and knights him. Exit* Pericles *at one door, and* Cleon *at another.*
>
> (Prol., II)

> *Enter* Pericles *and* Simonides *at one door, with Attendants; a Messenger meets them, kneels, and gives* Pericles *a letter;* Pericles *shows it* Simonides; *the Lords kneel to him. Then enter* Thaisa *with child, with* Lychorida, *a nurse; the King shows her the letter; she rejoices; she and* Pericles

take leave of her father, and depart [*with* Lychorida *and their Attendants. Then exeunt* Simonides *and the rest*].

(Prol., III)

The motions of the first dumb show are repeated almost exactly in the second up to the point of Thaisa's entrance, an interesting repetition since the first letter advises Pericles to flee and the second letter to return home. Common to each situation is the urgency of time's being short before disaster comes upon Pericles: in the first case, Helicanus reports Antiochus' plan to murder Pericles; in the second, Helicanus says that he will have to assume the crown if Pericles' absence from Tyre is prolonged. The brevity of the dumb show emphasizes the need for haste in each situation.

Still more significant, however, is the meaning of the stylized motions. Both occasions are ceremonial. Pericles, a displaced prince, takes his leave of rulers who are secure in their own lands. Circumstances outside of his control have limited his power to rule his land and he has lost the outward trappings of his royalty. The knighting of the Gentleman in the first pantomime and the kneeling of the Messenger and the Lords in the second visually proclaim Pericles' kingship and ratify his role as a "man on whom perfections wait" (I.i.80). Preceding the second dumb show is a scene at Tyre (II.iv) in which Helicanus refuses to accept the crown until the Lords search once more for Pericles, an action which reasserts the loyalty that Pericles commands. Pericles is seldom at the seat of his kingdom during the presented action, and only three scenes of the whole play occur in Tyre (I.ii and iii, II.iv). Still, the symbolic force of a harmonious kingdom conducted according to the just rule of a true prince is ever in the background as scene after scene displays a variety of discordant events. Pericles, as the true prince of Tyre, remains a constant value even in the mutable world of his travels. Thus, despite their narrative superfluity, the first two dumb shows present an important reminder through ritual that Pericles is potentially a just and a strong ruler.

The artificiality of an "antique" form is stressed a third way in the tournament scene (II.ii). The Entry of the knights onto the field and the Challenge are the most dramatic parts of a tournament, but in *Pericles* the playwright elaborated upon the less dramatic of the possibilities.[3] At Thaisa's birthday celebration, the scene displays the six knights from various countries in a deliberately static manner.[4] As each knight presents himself, Thaisa describes his shield with its emblematic device. The last is Pericles, who has retrieved his rusty armor from the sea, but who appears without squire or shield. His device is "a wither'd branch, that's only green at top; / The motto, *In hac spe vivo*" (II.ii.42–43).[5] The appropriateness of Pericles' device and motto extends further back than his recent recovery from the sea on the shores of Pentapolis. The reverberating context here, despite the interposition of several scenes at Tyre and Tharsus, is the opening scene at Antioch where Pericles risks his life for the hand of Antiochus' daughter. Amidst the skulls of former suitors who had failed to solve the riddle, Pericles commits himself in chivalric terms: "Like a bold

[3] See George R. and Portia Kernodle, "Dramatic Aspects of the Medieval Tournament," *Speech Monographs*, IX (1942), 163–72. In contrast to the use of the device in *Pericles*, consider the way in which the Challenge and the reported combat create suspense in *The Two Noble Kinsmen*.

[4] Comparison of this scene with a similar passing of military heroes in *Troilus and Cressida* (I.ii.200 ff.), where the man's bearing takes the place of a device and motto, shows how Shakespeare was able to use the expectations of such a convention to a very different purpose.

[5] Henry Green, *Shakespeare and the Emblem Writers* (London, 1870), 182, was unable to find Pericles' device in any of the emblem books that Shakespeare might have known and concludes that it was "invented by Shakespeare himself to complete a scene, the greater part of which had been accommodated from other writers." Hoeniger concurs, Arden edition, 56 n. 43.

champion I assume the lists" (I.i.62). The tournament of the first scene creates a grim background against which the health and vitality of Thaisa's "triumph" glow with hope. The field of the second tournament is peopled not with skeletons but with living men: Thaisa's love is not as costly as that of Antiochus' daughter. Whereas the first scene stresses the deadliness of the combat in which Pericles engages, the second tournament abbreviates the actual combat to an offstage shout, "*The mean Knight!*" The ritual of the tournament, which traditionally had been expressive of an harmonious society,[6] has been perverted in Antioch and is now restored in Pentapolis. Like his device, the withered branch that is green at the top, Pericles' tourneys have moved from death to life.

The use of ritualistic music in these two situations creates another contrast between the perverted kingdom of Antiochus and the harmonious rule of Simonides. Antiochus introduces his daughter with the order for "Music!" (I.i.6) and describes her as a bride fit for "Jove himself," which is hubristic self-flattery, in view of Gower's previous announcement that Antiochus has committed incest with her. Pericles describes her entrance as if she were a figure in a tableau and he were her presenter.

> See, where she comes apparell'd like the spring,
> Graces her subjects, and her thoughts the king
> Of every virtue gives renown to men!
> Her face the book of praises, where is read
> Nothing but curious pleasures, as from thence
> Sorrow were ever raz'd, and testy wrath
> Could never be her mild companion.
>
> (I.i.13–19)

---

[6] Kernodle and Kernodle, "Dramatic Aspects of the Medieval Tournament," 161.

Music frequently accompanied the unveiling of *tableaux vivants* in popular pageantry,[7] and in this scene Pericles' role as presenter offers an emblematic "progress" from innocent approbation to knowledgeable condemnation. Following his discovery of the riddle's meaning, he describes Antiochus' daughter in musical terms which imply a cosmological censure.

> You are a fair viol, and your sense the strings,
> Who, finger'd to make man his lawful music,
> Would draw heaven down and all the gods to hearken;
> But being play'd upon before your time,
> Hell only danceth at so harsh a chime.
>
> (I.i.82–86)

The moral and musical discord created by the entire episode at Antioch resolves into harmony with the banquet scene following Pericles' victory at Pentapolis. Pericles, conscious of his apparent inferiority in rank and modestly hesitant at first, finally agrees to take the place of honor beside the Princess Thaisa. As he sits with the king and the princess, he is struck by Simonides' resemblance to his own father in the former glory of his kingship. Realizing how far he is removed from such glory, Pericles becomes melancholy. Simonides publicly calls attention to Pericles' moodiness and proposes some "revels" to rouse him: two dances, the first a "soldier's dance" with all the knights in armor, and the second a mixed dance with knights and ladies.[8] Such dances,

---

[7] George Kernodle notes this echo of convention also; see his *From Art to Theatre: Form and Convention in the Renaissance* (Chicago, 1944), 139.

[8] John H. Long, "Laying the Ghosts in *Pericles*," *Shakespeare Quarterly*, VII (1956), 39–42, argues that the second dance is a duet between Pericles and Thaisa because this is his third test in the "arts of love." (See also Long's chapter on *Pericles* in *Shakespeare's Use of Music: The Final Comedies* [Gainesville, Fla., 1961], 35–49.) Hoeniger replies to Long's argument, Arden edition, 64–65 n. 106 S.D. He adds that in a play where so many stage directions are either missing or incomplete, there is little

appropriate to the masques James I enjoyed so much, symbolized the social harmony achieved under a just ruler.[9] The tournament scene and the "revels" scene in the hall of state thus combine two sequential rituals from royal pageantry into an emblem of harmony which resolves the discord of the opening scene of the play. The emblematic quality, rather than the dramatic potential, of the rituals is developed in both scenes, and this has caused critics to speculate that Shakespeare probably did not write them.[10] Yet it seems equally feasible that whoever the playwright was, he was striving to achieve a visual emblem in the opening acts of the play against which the final pattern of action could be measured.

Each device which I have discussed so far—Gower, the dumb show, the tournament, the ritual use of music and the dance—controls the audience in two important ways. First, the stress on artificiality asks them to consider the remoteness of the story from actual life. Second, the lack of dramatic development in the various scenes insists on a static, disconnected effect. Both of these effects create a conscious distance between the staged illusion and the audience. One result of this distance is to suggest a universal referent behind the particular action.[11] Another result is to shape a different way of looking at the play itself. Instead of seeing

reason to stress the absence of other Ladies in the revels scene. Simonides' praise of "all" following the second dance leads me to agree with Hoeniger's appraisal.

[9] John C. Meagher, *Method and Meaning in Jonson's Masques* (Notre Dame, Ind., 1966), 58–69, 82–91.

[10] Hoeniger, Arden edition, 62 n. 73–89, states that the dialogue of these two scenes (II.ii and iii), because of the undramatic repetition, makes them both "quite unShakespearean." See below, Appendix A, my discussion of the general problem of authorship in *Pericles*.

[11] Northrop Frye, *A Natural Perspective* (New York and London, 1965), 58, points out that "the effect of these archaizing tendencies in Shakespeare is to establish contact with a universal and world-wide dramatic tradition."

its parts as a developing dramatic continuum, we tend to see them as individual pictures. The effect resembles the one gained by looking at pictures in an exhibition or by reading through an emblem book. Each scene is a work of art, an entity in itself, and Gower acts as a guide who supplies the necessary links between each picture. As John Arthos suggests, the logic of the play is not so much in the progression of events as in the static, but incremental, framing of visual effects. Each episode presents an image which fills in a background for the final symbolic image of Pericles' waking to hear the music of the spheres.[12]

The first two acts may be considered to present a complete cycle of events: Pericles flees the evil at Antioch, aids the famine at Tharsus, is shipwrecked off the coast of Pentapolis, and wins the hand of Thaisa. The pattern of loss and restoration seems to be finally completed by Gower's Prologue and the dumb show which open Act III. Pericles' plans to return to Tyre and Thaisa's pregnancy both promise the comic order of a return to harmony. The parallels between the opening scene at Antioch and the scenes at Pentapolis which close Act II are important in creating the sense of a "rounded" action. Antiochus' trial of Pericles (I.i) threatens tragic consequences, but Simonides' mock trial of Pericles (II.v.) absorbs this tragic threat and resolves it, through comic treatment, into the harmonious conclusion of the betrothal.

The self-consciousness of the Pentapolis scene, however, calls specific attention to the limitations of the merely comic plot. That is, the Plautine comic plot is reduced in this scene to its logical absurdity. Simonides approves of Thaisa's choice to marry no one but Pericles, but when Pericles approaches, Simonides says that he "must dissemble it"

---

[12] John Arthos, *The Art of Shakespeare* (New York, 1964), 148–49.

(II.v.23). He then acts the role of "angry father" and raises nonexistent barriers for the young couple in love.[13] His hostility parodies the serious Antiochus, who had raised real barriers (though also arbitrary ones) for his daughter and Pericles. Simonides also parodies the comic role in the comic plot which he is enacting by turning it on its head. He forces the lovers to marry, whether or not it is their wish. Of course, he knows and the audience knows that they wish to marry. The scene's purpose in its immediate dramatic context is to prove to Pericles the nature of his own feelings; in its symbolic context, the scene reinstates Pericles' ability to trust in goodness beyond his own. But by calling attention to the limitations of the comic formula in this self-conscious way, the playwright is also suggesting that the comic resolution alone is insufficient to resolve the tragic complications which man faces. The later scene absorbs the earlier scene, but it does not blot it out. Just as its values qualify the obverse values of Antiochus, so the threat of evil embodied in Antiochus qualifies the promise of goodness in Simonides. That the action continues from this comic "resolution" is proof of its final inadequacy.

The events of the last three acts repeat and develop the pattern of loss and restoration established in the first two acts, yet the second cycle differs from the first. For one thing, Marina's confrontation with adversities is the focus of much of the later action up until the point of her reunion with Pericles. Her trials parallel her father's earlier ones, but she meets them differently. Her situation in the brothel scenes (IV.ii and vi) resembles in many ways Pericles' situation when he is tossed on to the shores of Pentapolis (II.i).

---

[13] Frye comments on the derivation of this role from the *senex iratus* of New Comedy; see *A Natural Perspective*, 74. There are clear similarities between Simonides in this scene and Prospero in *The Tempest*, especially in their mock opposition to the suitors for their daughters' hands.

Both scenes bring the main characters into an unidealized, unceremonial situation for the only time. Pericles' encounter with the fishermen and Marina's with the brothel-keepers allow them to develop dimensions of characterization which they would not otherwise have. In both situations, they have lost the protection of their royalty. Pericles tells the fishermen, "What I have been I have forgot to know; / But what I am, want teaches me to think on" (II.i.71–72). The problems are similar—how is Pericles to survive without means and without rank in a strange land, and how is Marina to preserve her chastity without means and without protection in a brothel?—but their solutions differ. Pericles survives because of the generosity of the people among whom he finds himself and Marina survives despite the animosity of her enemies.

Finding himself without royal power, Pericles is forced to reexamine his own nature. Does his rank determine his nature or is his nature real without rank, without his external role? The rusty armor which the fishermen retrieve from the sea permits Pericles to test himself in a royal context, but the rustiness distinguishes him from the other, well-accoutred knights. When he appears and the Lords comment on his "mean" apparel, Simonides remarks, "Opinion's but a fool, that makes us scan / The outward habit by [i.e., for] the inward man" (II.ii.55–56). The rusty armor is used primarily to signify the discrepancy between inner nature and outer form. (At Antioch, Pericles had painfully learned that outward form is not a sound basis for final judgment.) The fact that the armor became rusty in a matter of minutes is a temporal anachronism which places it outside the laws of verisimilitude and draws it into a realm of symbols. As Pericles listens aside, the fishermen discuss witnessing the shipwreck without being able to help the victims (II.i.18–19). Minutes later, the second fisherman draws the "rusty armour" from the sea in his net and Pericles claims it as his, given to him by his father in his will. The coincidence itself destroys the sense of verisimilitude, but the fact that the armor is already rusty takes the situation further outside the range of probability. Pericles' test of identity in the rusty armor takes on a parabolic tone even in a scene which is more realistic than most in the play.

Pericles is concerned with the testing of his identity in a philosophical way; Marina, however, has no doubts about her identity and no wish to test it in her new surroundings. Pericles is impressed with the fishermen's ability to draw a "pretty moral" from the life about them: "How from the finny subject of the sea / These fishers tell the infirmities of men" (II.i.48–49). Marina, however, finds nothing to admire in the cleverness of the brothel trio. The professions of the two groups are both practical methods to support themselves, but the difference is that one is honorable, providing food for man's necessary appetites, and the other dishonorable, providing food for man's supposedly controllable appetites. Each profession, nonetheless, is a practical business, and their common concern with practical matters—getting enough profit from their trade to avoid poverty—links them together as well as to another important scene in the play, the famine in Tharsus (I.iv). There is a dearth of wenches in Mytilene, a dearth of food in Tharsus. Pericles supplies the necessary food and relieves the famine; but Marina changes the demand for wenches to meet the decreased supply. Marina's incorruptible virtue, in other words, threatens to change the moral system in which a brothel can be a successful business. The parallelism involved in this set of scenes—the famine at Tharsus (I.iv), Pericles' rescue by the fishermen (II.i), and Marina's battle at the brothel (IV.ii and vi)—centers on the problem of human need and the ways in which it is met. Charity supplies the need for food and friendship; but adamantine virtue rigorously denounces sensual indulgence (IV.vi.162–68). Because he must depend on others for help and because this leads him to examine his own nature, Pericles is humanized by his experience with the fishermen. Marina, on the other hand, cannot afford to depend on the brothel inmates, and her nature remains absolute. The difference between Pericles' learning who he is and Marina's unshakable knowledge of her own identity is an important one because it keeps the audience engaged with Pericles' development even while they are attending to Marina's trials. Marina's story is a variation of Pericles', but she struggles against adversity and forces her situation to change. In contrast, Pericles accepts his reversals passively, finally withdrawing from the struggle of life altogether. Through the strength of her indefatigable nature, Marina reanimates the older generation with the spirit of youth.

A second distinction between the events in the last three acts and the pattern they reiterate from the first two acts is the creation of "wonder" both for Pericles and for the audience. The first two acts present wonderful events, but the understanding of those wonders remains muted until their meaning is experienced in Act V. For example, Pericles' affirmation of Providence when he recovers his father's armor—"I thank thee for 't; my shipwreck now's no ill, / Since I have here my father gave in his will" (II.i.132–33)— differs in resonance from his recognitions in the last act.

> O Helicanus, strike me, honour'd sir!
> Give me a gash, put me to present pain,
> Lest this great sea of joys rushing upon me
> O'erbear the shores of my mortality,
> And drown me with their sweetness.
>
> (V.i.190–94)

> This, this: no more. You gods, your present kindness
> Makes my past miseries sports.
>
> (V.iii.40–41)

These passages reveal development from a surface apprehension to a deep comprehension of the wonder that rests at the heart of experience. The wonder can be glimpsed (in the "rarest dream" [V.i.161]) or heard (in the heavenly "music of the spheres" [V.i.228]) only when the character's perceptive powers have been refined through repeated adversity.

The achievement of wonder for the audience is a matter of complex manipulations by the playwright. One method is the sacrifice of drama in scenes which precede Pericles' joyful recognition of Marina as his daughter. Ritual and visual symbol are stressed at every crucial turn of the plot. Dramatic tension, even when it is developed for a moment, is punctured quickly and never sustained. Consider, for example, the manner in which the storm at sea and the supposed death of Thaisa are presented. Gower's Prologue to Act III affirms the fact that Pericles and Thaisa followed Simonides' advice "with what haste you can, get you to bed." After a marriage feast of "pompous" proportions, when the company sleeps so soundly that only the cat waiting to catch the mouse and the crickets singing before the fire show signs of life,

> Hymen hath brought the bride to bed,
> Where by the loss of maidenhead
> A babe is moulded.
>
> (Prol., III.9–11)

Gower's description of the ritualized consummation, with its legendary tone, is quickly followed by the ritual dumb show, which brings Thaisa onstage "with child." The embarkation for Tyre and the storm which troubles the voyagers are all described, even with some elaboration, in Gower's opening sixty lines of the act. In another eighteen lines, Lychorida has told the "sea-tost Pericles" of Thaisa's death and has presented him with the baby, Marina. Everything happens so quickly that the audience hardly has time to respond with emotions of any fixity or magnitude.[14] The speed of the action from betrothal to death in childbirth allows Thaisa only symbolic characterization, and her distance from reality limits the degree to which the audience can become emotionally involved in her fate. Pericles and the sailors no sooner commit the coffined Thaisa to the sea than she is found on the shores of Ephesus and restored to life by Cerimon. Although Pericles cannot perceive the promise of ultimate reconciliation at this point, the audience can, and they are protected from anxiety about the outcome of this seeming catastrophe.

Thaisa's restoration provides the first significant experience of "wonder" in the play. Partially preparative and partially repetitive, it links the major segments of the play together. Just enough realistic causality remains to encourage acceptance of this event on a plane of probability—Thaisa was not actually dead when Pericles and the sailors thought so. Nonetheless, Cerimon is something of a magician, learned in the arts of healing, and he uses all the occult means at his disposal to awaken Thaisa from her deep and deathlike sleep. In a repetitive way, Cerimon's rousing of Thaisa recalls the lifting of Pericles from his melancholy through the revels at Simonides' court. In turn, the Pentapolis scene had reversed the negative effects of ritual in the opening scene at Antioch. These first actions (I.i and II.ii and iii), although symbolic in their ritualism, are grounded in the world of cause and effect. But Thaisa's recovery contains more of a mixture of the probable and the miraculous.

---

[14] Aside from the swiftness of action, Gower's stress upon the stage metaphor in his introduction to the scene mitigates our tragic sense of the action. Throughout the play Gower's tone is jocular, and because he conditions our responses, we are not allowed a fully tragic view of events.

Cerimon, like Antiochus, calls for music, but Cerimon uses it as a restorative rather than as a veil for evil. He calls for

> ... the fire and cloths.
> The still and woeful music that we have,
> Cause it to sound, beseech you. [*Music*]
> The viol once more; how thou stirr'st, thou block!
> The music there! [*Music*] I pray you, give her air.
> (III.ii.89–93)

And Thaisa lives again, first in her beginning to breathe ("See, how she 'gins to blow into life's flower again!"), then in motion (S.D., "*She moves*"), and at last in speech:

> O dear Diana,
> Where am I? Where's my lord? What world is this?
> (III.ii.107–108) [15]

We cannot fail to respond with the Gentlemen at the miracle of creation that this is "strange" and "most rare." Granted that Pericles erred in deeming Thaisa dead, her restoration nonetheless partakes of the miraculous world that Pericles later experiences himself in his own recovery from a deathlike apathy (V.i.160–63).

The Gentlemen in the scene of Thaisa's restoration are aware of Providential power guiding the world of the probable into its connection with the world of the improbable when they say to Cerimon, "The heavens, through you, increase our wonder" (III.ii.98). Pericles, too, is overwhelmed by the wonder of this fusion of worlds when the daughter he thought dead is miraculously restored to him. If man were in control of events, if his acts were alone the directors of consequence, then Marina would have died. Pericles recognizes that man's will is subordinate to Providential design,

---

15 Compare Thaisa's stages of recovery to those of Hermione in *The Winter's Tale* (V.iii).

and his perception sets him free from a world governed by
cause and effect. To Marina he says:

> Now, blessing on thee! rise; thou art my child.
> Give me fresh garments. Mine own, Helicanus,
> She is not dead at Tharsus, as she should have been,
> By savage Cleon.
>
> (V.i.212–15)

Pericles' recovery repeats with greater magnitude Thaisa's
recovery at Ephesus. Her restoration, in its turn, had developed the power of music hinted at in Pericles' earlier
awakening from melancholy at her father's court. The scene
at Ephesus is a symbolic ritual which affirms a central pattern of restoration, but in dramatic sequence it releases all
tension from Pericles' discovery of her at the end of the
play. The drama of Thaisa's loss is thus purposefully sacrificed to the symbolic meaning of her recovery as the scene
extends to join the first and the last of the play into a whole
fabric.

The method is not restricted to this scene; it is apparent in
other scenes which might as easily have been constructed to
exploit the dramatic conflict, but which were instead employed to enforce a symbolic point. An example occurs in
the sequence of Marina's abduction to Mytilene, a sequence
which some critics have found the most satisfactory drama
in the play.[16] The abduction itself is a form of anticlimax
which leaves the sinister figure of the murderer Leonine in
a rather comic position. He reiterates the threat of evil when
he returns to the stage after the pirates have left with Marina
(IV.i.99–102), but the fierceness of his threat has been un-
dermined by his readiness to run away the instant the pirates
appeared. The abduction thus punctures the tension of the

---

[16] See, for example, Hazelton Spencer, *The Art and Life of William
Shakespeare* (New York, 1940), 360–61.

proposed murder, and although Marina is led to a possible fate worse than death in Mytilene,[17] the release of tension in the abduction scene carries over a positive effect into the scenes at the brothel where the Bawd, Pandar, and Boult attempt to initiate Marina into their profession.

The brothel scenes present a real threat to Marina's virginity, but the threat is contained by comic treatment and by the contrast with the interposed scenes at Tharsus (IV.iii and iv). The treachery of Dionyza and Cleon in convincing Pericles that Marina is dead of natural causes makes the business partners of Mytilene's brothel seem open-handed by comparison. Everyone is powerless to assault Marina's virtue—even Boult, who determines to violate her just to keep the brothel in business. But Pericles falls to the deception of Dionyza and Cleon and withdraws into destructive apathy on his ship, dressed in sackcloth, and refuses to speak again. Following the segment at Tharsus, which returns Pericles to the proximity of the central action, is a scene that assures the audience they need not fear for Marina.

> [SCENE V.—*Mytilene*.]
> *Enter [,from the brothel,] two Gentlemen.*
> *1.Gent.* Did you ever hear the like?
> *2.Gent.* No, nor never shall do in such a place as this, she
>   being once gone.
> *1.Gent.* But to have divinity preach'd there! did you ever
>   dream of such a thing?
> *2.Gent.* No, no. Come, I am for no more bawdy-houses.
>   Shall's go hear the vestals sing?
> *1.Gent.* I'll do anything now that is virtuous; but I am out
>   of the road of rutting for ever. *Exeunt.*

[17] In Marina's eyes at least she is in a worse predicament than if Leonine had murdered her:

> Alack that Leonine was so slack, so slow!
> He should have struck, not spoke; or that these pirates
> Not enough barbarous, had not o'erboard
> Thrown me for to seek my mother!
>   (IV.ii.60–64)

This scene comically underscores the miraculous power of virtue: finding a virgin who preaches chastity in a brothel dislocates human expectations to such a degree that wonder is the chief response. This scene, like one in *The Winter's Tale* (V.ii), presents a comic referent for the serious enactment of wonder which is to follow in V.i. It creates an expectation of miracle at the same time it qualifies our response to it. Doubts about the credibility of such events are exorcised through laughter. The fullness of wonder is reserved for the climactic scene between Pericles and Marina, but the Gentlemen's testimonials prepare us to accept further evidences of Marina's remarkable power.

The scene with Lysimachus, the governor of Mytilene who comes to the brothel disguised,[18] affirms Marina's virtue so strongly that the Bawd and Boult fear for their profession. The Bawd implores Boult to "crack the glass of her virginity, and make the rest malleable" (IV.vi.142–43), and Boult approaches Marina to make her "go the way of

[18] Many critics have assumed that Lysimachus was a regular visitor to the brothel and that he experiences a conversion by talking with Marina. See, for example, G. Wilson Knight, *The Crown of Life* (London, 1965), 61–62. The reasons for his visit are left unexplained, although the Bawd and her associates have no doubts about what they were. Lysimachus denies that he came with "ill intent" and he responds to the brothel as to a diseased place. See his speeches, IV.vi.87–89, 103–104, 108–10, 118–20. There is no need to assume, as Knight does, that his asseverations about his good intentions are "shame-faced, though untrue." But see Philip Edwards, "An Approach to the Problem of *Pericles*," *Shakespeare Survey*, V (1952), 41–45. The dramatic importance of his visit, despite the unfortunate and probably unintentional problem it raises about his character, is that Marina's virtue is ratified by (presumably) the most reliable citizen of Mytilene. The characterization of Lysimachus in other scenes (V.i,iii) is very slight. In fact, Derek Traversi, *Shakespeare: The Last Phase* (Stanford, Calif., 1955), 42, misses his silent presence in the final scene at Ephesus and concludes that Marina is betrothed instead to Cerimon. This reading ignores Gower's announcement of Marina's betrothal to the "regent" of Mytilene (V.ii.8–11). It seems likely that the playwright wanted to use Lysimachus as a sound moral referent more than to call attention to his human corrigibility. Helicanus' comment to Pericles supports this view: "here's the regent, sir, of Mytilene, / Speaks nobly of her" (V.i.186–87).

women-kind." But Marina lashes him with her tongue to the point where Boult is more than happy to try to find work for her in more suitable surroundings, despite his lack of acquaintance among honest women.

The act ends with Boult's promise to help Marina, and Act V begins with Gower's narrative, stating that Boult's promise is fulfilled and Marina's escape accomplished.

> Marina thus the brothel 'scapes, and chances
> Into an honest house, our story says.
>
> (Prol., V.1–2)

This is hardly a dramatic escape. The villains succumb to the force of Marina's virtue and to her knowledgeable tongue that places values so accurately where they belong. The climax of the action is narrated rather than shown and this stresses the miraculous power of chastity that Marina has displayed in the brothel scenes. She is not so much endangered by the Bawd, Pandar, and Boult and their practical interests as their profession is endangered by the absolute power of her goodness.

The seriousness with which some critics read the brothel scenes ignores the important blending of tragic and comic perspectives. For example, John Arthos says, "The essential quality of the brothel scenes is their commonplaceness and their meanness. . . . This is the absence of poetry where little except cheapness is known. The attack upon Marina is thus more severe than anything Pericles has endured. . . . no one can intercede for Marina, no one can explain to her captors her right to her own desires." [19] This evaluation is partially accurate. But dramatically, that is, in the life of the scenes as they are acted onstage and in sequence, their comic

[19] Arthos, *The Art of Shakespeare*, 150–51. Another exclusively serious reading of this scene appears in Philip Edwards, *Shakespeare and the Confines of Art* (London, 1968), 141, 153–54.

quality is apparent and important. Certainly, Marina's virtue is stronger than Pericles', but this is not the only point these scenes make. The real threat is turned about and there is no contest. Virtue makes vice afraid. This is comic, not tragic, and it blends the impulses which operate together to unfold a new world where miracles are real, where good men live and evil men die, and where joy is an actual experience. The tragic threat of the brothel scenes, thus, is minimized through their comic treatment as well as through the nondramatic climax of the sequence.

In contrast to the absence of dramatic exploitation in this sequence, the scene in which the two story lines converge is highly dramatic. The fusion of the actual and dream worlds takes place at the moment of greatest tension in the play. Recognition between father and daughter is delayed as long as possible and is doubly effective because until this point other devices which might have achieved dramatic tensions have been so consciously underplayed. The scene begins with Lysimachus boarding Pericles' vessel in the Mytilene harbor. When Helicanus informs him of Pericles' distress, Lysimachus sends for Marina, whose "sweet harmony" of nature he is confident can restore Pericles. Marina sings, recalling Cerimon's use of music in the restoration of Thaisa, but Pericles does not immediately respond. She speaks to him and Pericles moves abruptly, apparently pushing her back.[20] She then poses a riddle that touches upon the heart of his disorder, and this rouses him to speak.

> *Mar.* I am a maid, . . .
> My lord, that, may be, hath endur'd a grief
> Might equal yours, if both were justly weigh'd.
> Though wayward fortune did malign my state,
> My derivation was from ancestors

[20] The stage direction is missing in the Quarto, but, as Hoeniger notes, lines 100 and 126 indicate the gesture.

> Who stood equivalent with mighty kings;
> But time hath rooted out my parentage,
> And to the world and awkward casualties
> Bound me in servitude. . . .

Per. My fortunes—parentage—good parentage—
To equal mine—was it not thus? what say you?

(V.i.84–98)

Pericles' gradual return to life is in marked stages, just as Thaisa's had been, and the wonder of the earlier miraculous recovery is now fully experienced and defined in Pericles' progressive recognition that this is, in fact, his daughter. Marina's revelation of her identity continues in the form of an incremental riddle, and Pericles' anxiety and hesitation to accept the truth behind the riddle recalls in an inverse way his immediate perception of the horrible truth behind Antiochus' riddle in the first scene. His delayed recognition of Marina builds a joyous anticipation of good that is greater because of the terrible knowledge of evil that has preceded it. The mutually regenerative power of Pericles' and Marina's relationship—"O, come hither, / Thou that beget'st him that did thee beget" (V.i.194–95)—replaces the cycle of death created by Antiochus and his daughter, who destroyed each other (I.i.65–72 and 128–34).

The joys which Pericles fears will "o'erbear the shores of my mortality, / And drown me with their sweetness" (V.i. 193–94) result from the fusion of his dream and reality. The "rarest dream" (161) and the "rarest sounds" (230) become a part of Pericles' actual experience, as real as the storms at sea and his previous hardships and suffering. Neither world obliterates the other, but each draws into the other forming a new reality which is fuller and more appropriate for a "vessel" that contains a mixture of the immortal with the mortal.[21]

21 The vessel imagery is a continuing metaphor which binds the parts

The center of concentration in this scene is Pericles' response to the miraculous fact that his daughter, whose tombstone he had seen in Tharsus, now lives. Unlike the audience in *The Winter's Tale*, who experience surprise with Leontes at Hermione's reanimation, we have previous knowledge that Marina lives. We are therefore free to watch intently the full impact of Pericles' recognition. Because he fears that his rising hopes will be shattered, Pericles resists accepting the knowledge that Marina is his. He is afraid that he is being "mock'd" by the gods (V.i.141–43) or by his own dream (V.i.161–62); and his disbelief of what we know is true forces us into a double awareness. Although we may have doubted the probability of Marina's story as we saw it performed, we have witnessed her history and we know that she is Marina. Any doubts we may have had concerning her history's probability have been allayed before this scene, and, when she says, "If I should tell my history, 'twould seem / Like lies, disdain'd in the reporting," we feel the need to defend her testimony. We therefore sympathize with Pericles' skepticism (we felt it ourselves previously) at the same time we are sure that the improbable is true. We affirm the miraculous because we have witnessed its improbable history. These contradictory impulses, to disbelieve and to

---

of the play together. There are, of course, the actual vessels on which and in which people travel, the casket of Thaisa, the ships of Pericles. And Gower describes the sorrowing Pericles thus: "He bears / A tempest, which his mortal vessel tears" (IV.iv.29–30). When Pericles recognizes that Antiochus' daughter is unchaste, he uses vessel imagery to describe her despoiled nature: "Fair glass of light, I lov'd you, and could still, / Were not this glorious casket stor'd with ill" (I.i.77–78). The common medieval and Renaissance association between man's life and a ship tossed on the sea of Fortune reaches back to classical tradition; and there is also a Biblical tradition which uses the vessel as an image of man: see especially Acts 9:15; Rom. 9:22; 1 Thess. 4:4; 2 Tim. 2:21; and 1 Pet. 3:7. The vessel image is frequent in all four of these plays in which men's lives are changed by sea journeys; and it is an especially appropriate image for the passivity of Pericles: he is the vessel chosen to demonstrate the final control of Providence in the realm of human action.

affirm what we know to be true, increase the pleasure of watching Pericles undergo the same contradiction. This is the peculiar catharsis that Shakespeare's tragicomedy creates, and the pleasure is only increased when we find that no one else in the play has seen the vision of Diana or heard the heavenly music of the spheres. With Pericles, we have witnessed these miracles.

The ritual of renewal, dramatically enacted, does overflow the "shores of mortality" and in the fusion of death and birth, dream and actuality, ritual and drama, the descent of a goddess into the world of man is an appropriate completion. Diana instructs Pericles to sail to Ephesus and to tell his story before her priestesses there (V.i.238–42). But while Pericles is fulfilling Diana's command, Gower intercedes with a brief summary of festivities in Mytilene and news of the betrothal of Marina and Lysimachus. The opening cycle of events had announced the betrothal of Pericles and Thaisa under the blessing of Simonides; the reiterative action includes the betrothal of Marina and Lysimachus under the blessing of Pericles. But the festive rituals and Pericles' entry into Mytilene are abbreviated now that the climax of dramatic action has passed, in contrast to the elaboration of the tournament and banquet ceremonies preceding Pericles' betrothal. For the second generation, the ritual is merely described, and Gower even apologizes for the narrative (V.ii.3–11).

The final scene of recognition between Pericles and Thaisa begins with a *tableau vivant* behind Gower as he speaks his last narrative. Thaisa stands as a High Priestess at Diana's altar with virgins on each side and Cerimon and the Ephesian citizens attending. Gower bridges the narrative distance between Mytilene and Ephesus and bids the audience watch the entry of the king and his train to the tableau already onstage.

Pericles announces himself and reviews his history, Thaisa recognizes him and faints, and, while Thaisa once more undergoes a restoration, Cerimon summarizes her story. The last recovery completes her former one, for although she had been returned to life by Cerimon, she had still to return to the full harmony of love with Pericles and Marina. Her swoon symbolically repeats the earlier deathlike sleep; and, like Pericles' withdrawal from life it prepares her to cross the "mortal shores" to a world in which boundaries have expanded to undetermined realms.

The harmony of this expanded world finds a final metaphor in Pericles' announcement that he and Thaisa shall return to govern Pentapolis, since Simonides has died, and that Lysimachus and Marina shall reign in Tyre. Tyre has throughout symbolized the harmony of a just rule, and the continuance of its prosperity under a new generation completes the motion of the play. All the locales of the play are included in the final harmony except for two, Antioch and Tharsus, places where evil has been perpetrated and divinely punished. In his Epilogue, Gower reiterates the important acceptance of Providential purpose with which Pericles' education has been concerned.

> In Pericles, his queen and daughter, seen,
> Although assail'd with fortune fierce and keen,
> Virtue preserv'd from fell destruction's blast,
> Led on by heaven, and crown'd with joy at last.
>
> (Epil., 3–6)

This play's achievement, like that of Shakespeare's other tragicomedies, is the experience of "joy"; and Gower leaves his audience with a blessing that transfers the play's joy to their own lives. If the dramatic illusion has succeeded in its purpose, the members of the audience discover in themselves a potential for miracle. For them, as well as for the characters of the play, the letting go, the submission of their will to a larger and greater director, opens the way to an emotional and imaginative health that is more than recovery—it is a new, more profound joy than they have been able to know.

Chapter III ❧ *CYMBELINE*
"A speaking such
as sense cannot untie"

To move from *Pericles* to *Cymbeline* is to move from majestic simplicity to bewildering complexity. *Cymbeline* has three basic plot lines, but each of these has many subsidiary plots and their interweaving is more intricate than the two plot lines in *Pericles*. First, there is the suit for the hand of Imogen, which includes Iachimo's "wager" and Cloten's "revenge" as well as Posthumus' banishment and return. A second plot concerns the lost sons of Cymbeline and their abductor-guardian Belarius; and the third is the separation and reunion of Britain and Rome. Furthermore, the chorus of *Pericles*, so artlessly open in the figure of Gower, becomes more integrated into the dramatic action in *Cymbeline*, although the choral speeches remain artificially obvious. For example, the Gentlemen of the opening scene supply the necessary background of Posthumus' lineage, the marriage of Imogen and Posthumus, and the earlier loss of the king's sons in set speeches that do not try to disguise their expository function (I.i.29–64).[1] Shakespeare has joined several conventional frameworks in *Cymbeline*, too, making the

[1] Other examples are Cornelius' speech to explain his substitution of a sleeping potion for poison (I.vi.33–44) and the Second Lord's recapitulation of what is wrong with the kingdom (II.i.54–67).

play more complicated in terms of audience expectations than *Pericles*. The earlier play is built primarily upon the romantic legend of a wandering hero who discovers that life's adversities have a benevolent purpose. *Cymbeline* also uses the romantic convention of the young hero banished from his homeland who finally returns to claim his heritage; but, in addition, *Cymbeline* incorporates the conventions of the history play and of the pastoral. Each of the three main plots, in fact, is a vehicle for one of these conventions: the romantic plot of New Comedy revolves about the Posthumus-Imogen relationship; the history play concerns the Britain-Rome controversy; and the pastoral conventions manifest themselves in the situation of Cymbeline's lost sons. Aside from this fusion of traditional expectations, characterization is more complex in *Cymbeline* than in *Pericles*. Posthumus fails to sustain his trust in Imogen and he suffers for his weakness; whereas Pericles suffers without commiting a sin. Because Posthumus errs, his heroic nature undergoes serious qualification. The censure which his lapse of faith and subsequent order for Imogen's murder incur is somewhat allayed, however, by the presence of Cloten who becomes a parodic surrogate for Posthumus both in life and in death. The interweaving of this triad of characterizations (Posthumus-Imogen-Cloten) is much more subtle and complicated than anything in *Pericles*.

Despite its greater complexity, *Cymbeline* resembles *Pericles* in its tragicomic action. Even though the main characters have a more intricate dramatic relationship, both Posthumus and Imogen undergo a reduction to "nothing" similar to Pericles' apathy before the restorative vision. Their settled sense of the world is dislocated and they rebuild their perspectives to include a much larger world than they had previously known. *Cymbeline* has also a great stress on artifice, and the mingling of tragic and comic "pleasures" has the same kind of effect as in *Pericles*. The sense of wonder in the final scene differs in several respects, but it is achieved through the double awareness of the characters and of the audience, all of whom are simultaneously involved in and removed from the staged illusion. *Cymbeline*, thus, shares with *Pericles* the chief characteristics of Shakespeare's tragicomic vision, but it displays a greater complexity of materials used to create that vision.

The discrepancy between man's true nature and his outward appearance, a theme developed to some extent in *Pericles*, becomes the dominant concern in *Cymbeline*. In the opening scene, the Gentlemen announce the problem: "You do not meet a man but frowns" (I.i.1). Cymbeline's anger is reflected in the faces of his subjects, but they are secretly glad that Imogen has married Posthumus rather than Cloten.

> But not a courtier,
> Although they wear their faces to the bent
> Of the king's looks, hath a heart that is not
> Glad at the thing they scowl at.
>
> (I.i.12–15)

This is the first of many dissembling countenances, but an important one. The king and his subjects do not feel the same way about the marriage of Imogen and Posthumus. Discord in the kingdom results from the enforced separation of the marriage partners. The harmony which a royal marriage of the king's only remaining child should effect is broken by the king's banishment of Posthumus; the dissembling looks of his lords, who are aware of Posthumus' superiority to Cloten, are a sign of the split between king and kingdom. The First Gentleman evaluates Imogen's two suitors candidly:

> *First Gent.* He that hath miss'd the princess is a thing
> Too bad for bad report: and he that hath her
> (I mean, that married her, alack good man,
> And therefore banish'd) is a creature such

> As, to seek through the regions of the earth
> For one his like; there would be something
>   failing
> In him that should compare. I do not think
> So fair an outward, and such stuff within
> Endows a man, but he.
> Sec. Gent.   You speak him far.
> First Gent. I do extend him, sir, within himself,
> Crush him together, rather than unfold
> His measure duly.
>
> (I.i.16–27)

This hyperbolic praise is immediately suspect, as the Second Gentleman indicates, but the arresting aspect—and a point that makes the praise hyperbolic—is that Posthumus seems as good within as he is outwardly fair. Such an evaluation is high praise indeed in a world which has grown used to discrepancies between the inner natures and outward appearances of men.

As the First Gentleman continues to present the history of Posthumus' lineage and birth, the Second Gentleman becomes so convinced that he must "honour him, / Even out of your report" (54–55). By this point, the death of Posthumus' father between his conception and birth and the death of his mother giving him birth have established Posthumus symbolically as the figure upon whom the life-from-death theme centers in the play. Posthumus' fame is known not only in Britain but in Rome as well. The guests in Philario's house speak of Posthumus' reputation in less worshipful tones (I.v) and so provide a balance for the hyperbole of the opening scene.

> Iach.   Believe it sir, I have seen him in Britain; he was
>   then of a crescent note, expected to prove so
>   worthy as since he hath been allowed the name of.
>   But I could then have look'd on him without the
>   help of admiration, though the catalogue of his

>   endowments had been tabled by his side and I to
>   peruse him by items.
> *Phil.*   You speak of him when he was less furnish'd than
>   now he is with that which makes him both with-
>   out and within.
> *French.* I have seen him in France: we had very many there
>   could behold the sun with as firm eyes as he.
> *Iach.*   This matter of marrying his king's daughter,
>   wherein he must be weighed rather by her value
>   than his own, words him (I doubt not) a great
>   deal from the matter.
> *French.* And then his banishment.
> *Iach.*   Ay, and the approbation of those that weep this
>   lamentable divorce under her colours are wonder-
>   fully to extend him; be it but to fortify her judge-
>   ment, which else an easy battery might lay flat,
>   for taking a beggar without less quality.
>
>   (I.v.1–23)

Iachimo's doubt that Posthumus could be as worthy as his reputation makes him seem characterizes Iachimo more than it does Posthumus; even so, his doubt polarizes the First Gentleman's assurance and suggests that the truth lies somewhere between the two evaluations. Philario's use of the word "furnish'd" suggests that acquiring the king's daughter in marriage has increased Posthumus' appearance of worth to match his inner nature. Iachimo immediately picks up the point and turns it to Posthumus' disadvantage, a comment which increases the distance between Philario's open-natured hospitality and Iachimo's capacity for distorting appearances. Still, the idea of Imogen as a furnishing carries preparative weight for the wager which follows. In agreeing to test Imogen's pure spirit, Posthumus unwittingly gives evidence that he views her as an object to be possessed rather than as a person to be known by her own identity. The wager which symbolizes his limited perspective fits appropriately into a scene which qualifies his good report.

From this point, the central action in the play concerns Posthumus' growing inwardly to match his noble outward appearance.

Posthumus' reported worth is entwined with Imogen's esteem of him in both of these scenes. Iachimo's recognition that Posthumus' marriage to the king's daughter weighs greatly in his favor (I.v.14–25) echoes the First Gentleman's most convincing proof of Posthumus' worth:

> To his mistress,
> (For whom he now is banish'd) her own price
> Proclaims how she esteem'd him; and his virtue
> By her election may be truly read
> What kind of man he is.
>
> (I.i.50–54)

As heir apparent, Imogen's "price" is absolute without the additional force of her own worthy nature to support her value. As she herself recognizes, the fact that she is the only heir to the throne makes her price more important than her desires are.

> Had I been thief-stolen,
> As my two brothers, happy: but most miserable
> Is the desire that's glorious. Bless'd be those,
> How mean soe'er, that have their honest wills,
> Which seasons comfort.
>
> (I.vii.5–9)

> 'Mongst friends?
> If brothers: [*Aside*] would it had been so, that they
> Had been my father's sons, then had my prize
> Been less, and so more equal ballasting
> To thee, Posthumus.
>
> (III.vii.47–51)

Both of these speeches express Imogen's wish to realize her true nature—always in conjunction with Posthumus—together with her understanding that her role as Cymbeline's daughter forces a discrepancy between her inner and outward natures. The latter speech occurs when she has disguised her appearance in order to seek Posthumus. She knows that he has ordered her murder, but she also knows that her identity is merged with his. Her recognition that she is, against her will, a pawn in Cymbeline's world, which is also the world she has to live in, pathetically underlines the use of her as an object in the wager between Iachimo and Posthumus. Her reputation, however, is the thing wagered upon, not her inner nature, although Posthumus assumes there is no difference. The outward Imogen is all that Posthumus knows as yet, but insofar as her inner nature depends upon him, the inner Imogen is inextricably limited by her "report." She must give the lie to her appearance, finally, in order to save the value of her real identity from destruction.

The wager grows out of a circumstance similar to one that Posthumus had encountered during earlier travels in France. He had, on a former occasion, been about to duel in defense of his lady's honor when a Frenchman, who is now a guest in Philario's house, had persuaded the two rash men to desist. Posthumus' testiness on the subject is immediately apparent when he bristles at the Frenchman's implication that the matter was too slight to risk death over. Iachimo, quick to notice Posthumus' vulnerability, inquires further into the cause of the proposed duel, and cynically avows that perfection in ladies is a state unknown in this world. Posthumus takes the bait and is drawn into the wager easily enough, despite his statement that his lady's virtue "is not a thing for sale, and only the gift of the gods" (I.v. 87–88). Philario protests with the voice of reason that the wager rose too suddenly and should be left to "die as it was born" (125), but Iachimo pushes and Posthumus bends, putting up the ring which he has sworn he would wear on his finger "while sense can keep it on" (I.ii.49). Obviously his reason has given way to his pride of purchase for that which cannot be bought.

The ignobility of encouraging a test of Imogen's virtue does not occur to Posthumus, and he is only aware of how his own sense of honor has been pricked by Iachimo's boasts. Posthumus' lack of insight becomes even clearer to the audience, however, in the scene which soon follows where Iachimo actually tests Imogen's virtue. When he first views her, Iachimo perceives that he may be in for a real test of his own power of deception.

> [*Aside*] All of her that is out of door most rich!
> If she be furnish'd with a mind so rare,
> She is alone th' Arabian bird; and I
> Have lost the wager.
>
> (I.vii.15–18)

There is a verbal as well as conceptual parallel in this evaluation which recalls Philario's comment that Posthumus is more furnished now with that "which makes him both without and within" (I.v), and the meaning of Philario's statement is enhanced by this elaboration. Imogen has a mind as rare as her beauty and being so "furnish'd" she can supply Posthumus with what he may lack in making the inner and outward man the same. That she is more nearly concordant in her inner and outer natures is clear from the manner in which she resists Iachimo's testimony that Posthumus has been false to her in Rome. When Iachimo encourages her to revenge Posthumus' infidelity by allowing him to her bed, Imogen recognizes his utter baseness.

> Away, I do condemn mine ears, that have
> So long attended thee. If thou wert honourable,
> Thou wouldst have told this tale for virtue, not
> For such an end thou seek'st, as base, as strange.

Thou wrong'st a gentleman, who is as far
From thy report as thou from honour, and
Solicits here a lady that disdains
Thee, and the devil alike.

(I.vii.141–48)

Imogen does not hesitate, when her reason distinguishes
Iachimo's lies, to discount them as in any way affecting
Posthumus' real nature. Posthumus, on the other hand, does
not even demand all the evidence that Iachimo has collected
to condemn Imogen of infidelity. Her assurance of his goodness and his assurance that she has been false are a measure
of the distance that he has yet to travel before he is in fact
worthy of her.

When Iachimo shows the stolen bracelet which Posthumus had given Imogen at his departure and which signified her fidelity, just as the diamond ring which Posthumus
had put up for the wager signified his, Posthumus immediately assumes the worst has happened.

Here, take this too;

                           [Gives the ring.
It is a basilisk unto mine eye,
Kills me to look on't. Let there be no honour
Where there is beauty: truth, where semblance: love,
Where there's another man. The vows of women
Of no more bondage be to where they are made
Than they are to their virtues, which is nothing.
O, above measure false!

(II.iv.106–13)

Philario persuades him to ask for more than this circumstan-
tial evidence, advising patience, but when Iachimo swears
he "had it from her arm" Posthumus again relaxes into ig-
noble doubt. Philario, acting Posthumus' part in defense of
Imogen, forces Iachimo to give further evidence of Imogen's
guilt and Iachimo reveals his knowledge of the mole under

her breast. Despite the seriousness of the consequences of his belief in Iachimo's lies, Posthumus' eagerness to accept them without even reasonable questioning places him in a foolish position, so that when he returns at the end of the scene to deliver his diatribe against women, his excess spills over from a tragic to a comic effect. Posthumus, the fool, does not measure consistently with the image of his worth built up at the play's beginning.

Cloten, the true fool, makes Posthumus' deficiencies as a romantic hero even more apparent when he dons Posthumus' clothes and parodies Posthumus' violent speech with a diatribe of his own (IV.i). Yet by his very violence, which is more gratuitous than Posthumus' bitter reaction to Iachimo's lies, Cloten takes some of the censure away from Posthumus. In fact, Cloten repeatedly "protects" Posthumus' characterization as he absorbs criticism through his excessive and parodic actions. Their characters regularly qualify each other, either in the report of others or in Cloten's conversation, yet they never appear onstage together. In the first scene, during the Gentlemen's discussion of Imogen's choice, the First Gentleman says bluntly enough that Cloten "is a thing / Too bad for bad report" (I.i.16–17). And after Posthumus has appeared onstage and departed, Cymbeline berates Imogen for her choice. She replies with some force that "I chose an eagle, / And did avoid a puttock" (I.ii.70–71). In the wake of Posthumus' noble report and noble appearance, Cloten's report suffers comic diminution. Pisanio adds another facet to Cloten's already clownish characterization when he tells the Queen and Imogen of how Cloten detained the banished Posthumus by drawing upon him. Pisanio states that if Posthumus had not played, but fought, Cloten would have suffered injury. Imogen's anger at Cloten's indecorous action flares.

Your son's my father's friend, he takes his part
To draw upon an exile. O brave sir!
I would they were in Afric both together,
Myself by with a needle, that I might prick
The goer-back.

(I.ii.96–100)

Imogen's scorn for Cloten, which never alters while he lives, expresses itself through comparative means. She implies, as the First Gentleman has, that to yoke Cloten and Posthumus in the same breath, or worse, to join them in any comparison, is an act that disturbs reason. No real comparison is possible: the eagle resembles the puttock only in species.

Thus introduced, Cloten appears onstage with two Lords, who make their distaste for him farcically clear.

First Lord. Sir, I would advise you to shift a shirt; the violence of action hath made you reek as a sacrifice: where air comes out, air comes in: there's none abroad so wholesome as that you vent.

Clo. If my shirt were bloody, then to shift it. Have I hurt him?

Sec. Lord. [*Aside*] No, faith: not so much as his patience. . . .

Clo. I would they had not come between us.

Sec. Lord. [*Aside*] So would I, till you had measur'd how long a fool you were upon the ground.

Clo. And that she should love this fellow, and refuse me!

Sec. Lord. [*Aside*] If it be a sin to make a true election, she is damn'd.

(I.iii.1–7, 21–27)

To tell a prince that he smells bad is a grievous breach of decorum, yet Cloten fails to comprehend it. His refusal to change his shirt unless it were bloody characterizes his oblivious offensiveness. He cannot sense much in the way of social delicacy and he comprehends nothing of the way he affects others. The broadness of the Second Lord's jests is another measure of how far Cymbeline has inverted the proper order of his kingdom and forced a division between appearance and reality. A comic butt is hardly a match for a princess of Imogen's rare understanding.

The next scene in which Cloten and his pair of Lords appear (II.i) reveals further his bad temper at losing, this time at the game of bowls. To express his anger, Cloten has broken his bowl over a spectator's head. Through his comments on the observance of decorum, Cloten shows himself to be even more stupid and childish than he has seemed already. In attempting to observe proper form, Cloten creates self-parody, and, as always, he is oblivious to the foolish impression he makes. "I had rather not be so noble as I am," he says, annoyed because his inferiors refuse to fight with him. He considers it "fit I should commit offence to my inferiors" and inquires if it is "fit I went to look upon" the stranger, Iachimo, who has come to court. The Second Lord again toys with him in some rather broad punning, assuring Cloten that it would be impossible for him to "derogate" himself by any action. The soliloquy which this Lord remains onstage to speak, however, suggests the more serious attitude that informs the disgruntled courtiers' comic dissembling.

> That such a crafty devil as is his mother
> Should yield the world this ass! a woman that
> Bears all down with her brain, and this her son
> Cannot take two from twenty, for his heart,
> And leave eighteen. Alas poor princess,
> Thou divine Imogen, what thou endur'st,
> Betwixt a father by thy step-dame govern'd,
> A mother hourly coining plots, a wooer
> More hateful than the foul expulsion is
> Of thy dear husband, than that horrid act
> Of the divorce, he'ld make. The heavens hold firm

The walls of thy dear honour, keep unshak'd
That temple, thy fair mind, that thou mayst stand,
T' enjoy thy banish'd lord and this great land!

(II.i.54–67)

The soliloquy acts also as a bridge from the low comedy to
the awe-inspiring scene in Imogen's bedchamber, where Iachimo gathers signs of her beauty to use in his deception of
Posthumus. The divinity which the Second Lord attributes
to Imogen is immediately confirmed by Iachimo's description of what he sees: "Though this a heavenly angel, hell is
here" (II.ii.50). The admiration which the Second Lord and
Iachimo express for Imogen's nature and outward beauty
finds its terms in a theological vocabulary. To the Second
Lord, Imogen is "divine," and he prays that the "heavens"
will protect her honor and the "temple" of her mind. Iachimo describes her very breath as "perfume," an incense
for the "chapel" which her chamber seems to him. His own
monstrous purpose frightens him as he commits the sacrilege
of plundering a shrine. Although he fails to realize that he
alone creates the "hell" which "is here," he perceives the
monstrous contrast between Imogen, "a heavenly angel,"
and the lie he intends to give of her.

This awed use of a theological vocabulary to describe the
perfections of the human Imogen complements the punning
use of it in earlier scenes. Both Imogen and the Second Lord
indulge in theological punning in the scenes which reveal
their repugnance for Cloten. This word play reverberates
against a system of values that involves more than a local
crisis in Cymbeline's kingdom: the values concern the spiritual nature of man himself. When Imogen resists her father's
advancement of Cloten, Cymbeline accuses her of heaping
age upon him when she should repair his youth. She responds that she is senseless of his wrath because "a touch
more rare / Subdues all pangs, all fears."

Cym.   Past grace? obedience?
Imo. Past hope, and in despair, that way past grace.
                                                (I.ii.66–68)

Again, when Imogen questions Pisanio about Posthumus' departure, she says, "if he should write, / And I not have it, 'twere a paper lost / As offer'd mercy is" (I.iv.2–4). And when she laments her lack of free choice, Imogen creates a tenth Beatitude: "Bless'd be those, / How mean soe'er, that have their honest wills, / Which seasons comfort" (I. vii.7–9).[2] Her loss of Posthumus—though at this point only through physical banishment rather than through his betrayal of spirit, which occurs later—she regards at least metaphorically as a loss of heavenly grace and the possibility of redemption. When the Second Lord jestingly concurs that "if it be a sin to make a true election, she is damn'd" (I.iii. 26–27), he pinpoints two problems of perspective. First, according to Cymbeline's inverted order, Imogen is damned—by her choice to live outside of Cymbeline's grace, and by his choice for her to be besieged by Cloten. Second, Imogen herself has substituted Posthumus for the ultimate values her soul can achieve. He is her source of grace, the means to her redemption. She learns, in the course of the play, how great a risk she incurs by this substitution for her own sense of being, and she too finds a more inclusive referent for her own identity. The final goal of romance conventions proves insufficient for her as well as for Posthumus. Such serious issues are only implied by the theological vocabulary, and they are contained by their punning usage. Taken with absolute seriousness, they would push beyond the delicate balance of tragicomedy; but their inclusion through the rhetoric of comedy provides a reminder that Shakespeare's tragicomic

---

[2] Compare the poetic rhythms of the Beatitudes from Christ's Sermon on the Mount, Matt. 5:3–11.

vision is firmly anchored in meaningful issues. The use of a
theological vocabulary and the spiritual concerns which it
implies deepen the characterizations of both Imogen and
Posthumus in marked contrast to the surface characterization of Cloten.[3]

In the very next scene, following Iachimo's enchanted description of the sleeping Imogen, Cloten impatiently says,
"If I could get this foolish Imogen, I should have gold
enough" (II.iii.7–8). His reduction of Imogen to a foolish
girl and to an object of barter comically qualifies his own
powers of perception; at the same time, it comments upon
the use of Imogen as an object of barter by Cymbeline, by
Posthumus, and by Iachimo. All three of these men are
drawn into a comic conflation with Cloten at this moment
of his imperception. His attempt to "penetrate" Imogen
with a morning song further demonstrates his superficial
level of understanding. The contrast between the boorish
Cloten and the delicate task of the music to appeal to Imogen
on his behalf illustrates how art itself can be violated. The
aubade has an ideal artistic purpose, to celebrate the morning and love, and its use by appropriately noble romantic
characters (such as Romeo and Juliet) realizes its conventional beauties; but used by Cloten, it becomes "too much
pains / For purchasing but trouble" (II.iii.89). That it fails
is not the fault of the music, as Cloten would interpret it,
but the fault of those who promote the music in hopes that
it will have an aphrodisiac effect on the "stern" Imogen
(II.iii.37).[4] This scene modulates the tone between the bed-

[3] Imogen's application of the theological terms *grace* and *mercy* to
Posthumus underlines the dramatic irony created by his lack of generosity.
Posthumus' want of Patience and his learning to delay judgment consti-
tute the poles of his spiritual journey. Concerning the theme of Patience
and the education of the human spirit, see Robert G. Hunter, *Shakespeare
and the Comedy of Forgiveness* (New York and London, 1965), Chap. 1.

[4] See Eric Partridge's note under "penetrate" in *Shakespeare's Bawdy*
(New York, 1960), 163. The word *penetrate* has special meaning in Re-

chamber scene, in which Imogen is described in terms of divinity, and her confrontation with Cloten in which she expresses her distaste for him in vitriolic terms; but it is also a criticism of the improper uses of art.[5] The harmony of art results from appropriate human motivations, and perversion here as well as in other actions characterizes Cloten's ineffectual malice.

So far is Cloten from achieving success with his music that Imogen "vouchsafes no notice" (II.iii.41). Still, on the advice of the Queen, Cloten pursues Imogen to her chamber, parodically repeating Iachimo's earlier pursuit of her. Imogen's strained tolerance breaks under Cloten's persistence in his suit and his denigration of Posthumus.

> *Imo.*   Profane fellow,
> Wert thou the son of Jupiter, and no more
> But what thou art besides, thou wert too base
> To be his groom: thou wert dignified enough,
> Even to the point of envy, if 'twere made
> Comparative for your virtues to be styled
> The under-hangman of his kingdom; and hated
> For being preferr'd so well.
> *Clo.*   The south-fog rot him!
> *Imo.* He never can meet more mischance than come
> To be but nam'd of thee. His mean'st garment,
> That ever hath but clipp'd his body, is dearer

naissance theories of music as well as a sexual implication. For discussion, see Gretchen L. Finney, "Ecstasy and Music in Seventeenth-Century England," *Journal of the History of Ideas*, VIII (1947), 175 ff.; and James Hutton, "Some English Poems in Praise of Music," *English Miscellany*, II (1951), 20 ff.

5 Richmond Noble, *Shakespeare's Use of Song* (London, 1923), 130–35, makes several perceptive points about this aubade. He suggests that because of the limitations of his theater Shakespeare used the morning song as a means to transform night into dawn. Noble does not consider the possibility of the indoor lighting advantages of the second Blackfriars theater which the King's Men had leased by the probable dates of composition of *Cymbeline*. For further comments on the song, see J. M. Nosworthy, Arden edition, *Cymbeline* (London, 1964), Appendix C, 220–22.

In my respect, than all the hairs above thee,
Were they all made such men.

(II.iii.125–37)

Cloten grasps the insult of "the mean'st garment" and repeats it several times throughout the remaining action of the
scene while Imogen directs Pisanio to search for her missing
bracelet. Cloten's sense of injury irritates Imogen so much
that she offers to satisfy him with a duel. He replies with a
threat to tell her father and she leaves, obviously in disgust. Cloten remains onstage to say, "I'll be reveng'd: / 'His
mean'st garment!' Well."

With all the power of his one-track mind, Cloten pursues
his revenge by wearing Posthumus' garments—though not
his meanest ones.[6] After several scenes in which he appears,
comically, as counselor to the king advising him to defy
Rome, and as wretched lover in the Catullian fashion (III.v.
71–81), he directs Pisanio to bring him some of Posthumus'
garments. Cloten ruminates to himself:

> She said upon a time (the bitterness of it I now belch from
> my heart) that she held the very garment of Posthumus in
> more respect than my noble and natural person; together
> with the adornment of my qualities. With that suit upon
> my back, will I ravish her: first kill him, and in her eyes;
> there shall she see my valour, which will then be a torment
> to her contempt. He on the ground, my speech of insult-
> ment ended on his dead body, and when my lust hath
> dined (which, as I say, to vex her I will execute in the
> clothes that she so prais'd) to the court I'll knock her back,
> foot her home again. She hath despis'd me rejoicingly, and
> I'll be merry in my revenge.

(III.v.132–50)

[6] The intricate irony of the parodic relationship between Cloten and
Posthumus manifests itself here. When Posthumus puts on the clothes of
a British peasant to fight the invading Romans (V.i.23–24), he is most
worthy of Imogen's praise. He is most noble when dressed in his "mean'st
garment."

The brutality of his intentions for the first time outweighs the comedy of his position and his departure for Milford-Haven sets a real threat into motion. The expression of his enthusiasm to gain his revenge (III.v.159–60) echoes Imogen's eager departure for the same place, where she deludedly thought she would find her loving husband (III.ii. 49). Both Imogen and Cloten rush to their imagined fulfillment with energy that finds its answer in death: for Imogen, only in seeming, but for Cloten, in actuality.

From this point on, Cloten and Imogen are symbolically linked because they are both disguised: Cloten wears Posthumus' clothes and Imogen wears those of a page. The changes in appearance create odd confusions, but for the audience the inner natures of the characters never alter. Imogen in her soliloquy before the cave of Belarius and the two brothers is very much herself, despite her altered situation (III.vi). She has learned a new perspective—"I see a man's life is a tedious one"—but her reflections on the shifting values of her world show her to be absorbing new experience with her characteristically full understanding. Two scenes later Cloten, alone on the same bare stage near the cave, offers his soliloquy of malice and revenge. He is still puzzling over the problem of why Imogen prefers Posthumus to him: "The lines of my body are as well drawn as his; no less young, more strong, not beneath him in fortunes, beyond him in the advantage of the time, above him in birth, alike conversant in general services, and more remarkable in single oppositions; yet this imperseverant thing loves him in my despite. What mortality is!" (IV.i.10–16). Imogen's poetic contemplation of possible deception even in poor folk who only give directions (III.vi.8–14) suggests a complexity of perception that renders Cloten's simple assurance comic. In prose, he speaks also of directions he has been given: "the fellow dares not deceive me" (IV.i.27). Her sensitivity to ambiguity in appearances and his oblivion to it join them in a parodic duet which culminates in their common burial.

Having befriended Belarius and the two brothers, Imogen remains behind in their cave while they go out to hunt. Because she feels sick, she takes the sleeping potion that has found its devious way to her from the Queen. No sooner has Imogen retired to the cave than Cloten enters, also feeling "faint" (IV.ii.63). Belarius recognizes him and fears that he must be accompanied by others from the court. Guiderius tells the other two to look for Cloten's "companies" and takes on the irate prince alone. Their exchange is humorous more than foreboding and Cloten manages to seem typically pompous and foolish. Their dialogue (IV.ii.74–100) insists on comparisons, not only between Cloten and his adversary, Guiderius, and between Cloten and Posthumus, whose clothes he wears, but also between what Cloten claims to be—a prince—and what he is—a fool. A few lines later the fool is beheaded, but his power to elicit laughter remains in his "report." Cloten has found concord between his inner and outer natures only as a dead fool. Horror is impossible, even in response to the spectacle of Cloten's head severed from its body. When Guiderius explains the battle, the audience can only nod at the appropriateness of Cloten's end; he had found nothing so "fit" at court.

> Gui.   With his own sword,
> Which he did wave against my throat, I have ta'en
> His head from him: I'll throw't into the creek
> Behind our rock, and let it to the sea,
> And tell the fishes he's the queen's son, Cloten,
> That's all I reck.
>
> (IV.ii.149–54)

The severed head floating down the "creek" to the sea is strongly reminiscent of the "Death of Orpheus" in Ovid's *Metamorphoses* (XI, 50 ff.), but with a parodic diminution.

Cloten's association with music in the presentation of a morning song to Imogen establishes his perversion of the art. His death and dissolution in this mock-heroic conclusion, which he himself predicted would be Posthumus' fate at his own hands (IV.i.17–18), is an appropriate ending for the fool whose sole effect has been to invert. Cloten, the anti-Orpheus, in death fulfills the purpose he vainly attempted to realize in his life: that is, he assumes the outward nobility he has always claimed he possessed. Without his head, which when attached testified to his lack of reason, Cloten actually differs little from the "noble" Posthumus.

Imogen, upon waking next to the headless body of Cloten dressed in Posthumus' garments, assumes that this is in fact her murdered husband.

> The dream's here still: even when I wake it is
> Without me, as within me: not imagin'd, felt.
> A headless man? The garments of Posthumus?
> I know the shape of's leg: this is his hand:
> His foot Mercurial: his Martial thigh:
> The brawns of Hercules: but his Jovial face—
> Murder in heaven! How?—'Tis gone. . . .
> . . . Damn'd Pisanio
> Hath with his forged letters (damn'd Pisanio)
> From this most bravest vessel of the world
> Struck the main-top!
>   (IV.ii.306–12, 317–20)

Imogen's confusion of Cloten's body with that of her husband's seems offhand to be an outrageous flaunting of probability.[7] Yet the shock of identification of two polarized figures, the fool and the hero, forces the audience to puzzle over its plausibility. Suddenly, all the pretenses to real dis-

---

[7] Harley Granville-Barker, *Prefaces to Shakespeare*, Second Series (3 vols.; London, 1927–36), II, 246–47, points out that the "emphasizing of the artifice . . . does much to mitigate the crude horror of the business, to bring it into the right tragi-comic key."

tinctions which depend on outward form have been exploded. Posthumus, without the distinction of rational perception and rational control of his appetites, might very well be a Cloten. The missing head symbolizes the vast difference between them, yet Posthumus has already displayed his capacity for unreason in response to Iachimo's lies about Imogen.

The identification of Cloten and Posthumus has been very carefully and pointedly prepared for by Cloten's insistence that there was little physical difference between them. And though the audience tends to disregard the validity of Cloten's insistence upon this point, when the identification occurs, we immediately recognize its truth and proceed to evaluate its implications. It is not, as some critics claim, evidence of Imogen's stupidity, but instead it is a device to enforce the essential perception that outward seeming and inner being have a complex relationship which formulas of any kind tend to oversimplify. The Posthumus of noble and worthy report exists until he is subjected to a test of faith; however, that "noble" Posthumus is not destroyed because he fails the test. The identity of outer and inner worthiness is still possible, but it has to be achieved through adversities that challenge the character's potential worth to awaken and to realize itself.

The death of Cloten and Imogen's confusion of his headless body with Posthumus provide a symbolic and dramatic link to the next appearance of Posthumus onstage.[8] Cloten

[8] Some critics, of whom Nosworthy is typical, feel that Posthumus' long absence from the stage is not overcome successfully by his return in Act V: his appearance is not integrated into the dramatic flow of events (Arden edition, 152 n.). However, Posthumus' physical absence from the stage has been more than balanced by the fact that he has been the central focus of almost all the other characters' thoughts and actions (with the exception of those of the Roman ambassador and party). In addition, the death of Cloten brings Posthumus onstage in effect, even though by substitution.

has become a surrogate victim for Posthumus and in his death has absorbed much of the blame which otherwise would still attach to Posthumus' figure. Imogen's lament over what she thinks is Posthumus' body and her bathing her cheeks in his blood (IV.ii.330) cleanses the figure of Posthumus of the worst of his blame, so that when he enters soon thereafter (V.i) the audience is prepared to accept his own lament with sympathy. The fact that Posthumus carries a blood-soaked handkerchief, sent to him by Pisanio at his command as evidence of Imogen's death, links his lament with Imogen's visually and symbolically. They are both deceived by surrogate victims, but the reality of death makes clear to each of them what true values the other held for them. The evidences of infidelity, which have convinced them that each has been deceived by the other, no longer weigh significantly in their feelings. The more substantial values of their union have clarified themselves and symbolically prepare them for their ultimate reconciliation. With the death of Posthumus, Imogen confronts "nothing." In reply to Caius Lucius' question "What art thou?" she says, "I am nothing; or if not, / Nothing to be were better" (IV.ii.366–67). And Posthumus dedicates himself to "die / For thee, O Imogen, even for whom my life / Is, every breath, a death" (V.i. 25–27). Their former identities have been tested by crisis and the surfaces of their natures have been shattered, so that they must rebuild themselves out of core substance.

At this point Posthumus too dons a disguise in order that his true nature will not be hampered by his outward appearance.

> I'll disrobe me
> Of these Italian weeds, and suit myself
> As does a Briton peasant: so I'll fight
> Against the part I come with: so I'll die
> For thee, O Imogen, even for whom my life

Is, every breath, a death: and thus, unknown,
Pitied, nor hated, to the face of peril
Myself I'll dedicate. Let me make men know
More valour in me than my habits show.
Gods, put the strength o' th' Leonati in me!
To shame the guise o' th' world, I will begin,
The fashion less without, and more within.

(V.i.22–33)

The pointed reversal of the final couplet can hardly be missed. Whereas in the first scene of the play the appearance of nobility was the starting point in both Posthumus' report and actions—that is, his actions were directed toward supporting his outward guise—now he will act from inner nobility and force the outward fashion to coincide with the inner man. As in the "rusty armour" episode in *Pericles*, base appearance will henceforth be associated with noble action and change the "guise o' th' world."

Posthumus is not the only one to suggest that the world's habit of equating noble appearance with noble action is misleading. The two sons of Cymbeline in their wild and savage environment have acted so gently toward Imogen that she remarks: "These are kind creatures. Gods, what lies I have heard! / Our courtiers say all's savage but at court; / Experience, O, thou disprov'st report!" (IV.ii.32–34). The valiant brothers and Posthumus come together in the battle scene to save Cymbeline from the Romans and together with Belarius they are the talk of the British soldiers (V.iii.84–87) and of the court group.

Cym. Stand by my side, you whom the gods have made
    Preservers of my throne: woe is my heart,
    That the poor soldier that so richly fought,
    Whose rags sham'd gilded arms, whose naked breast
    Stepp'd before targes of proof, cannot be found:
    He shall be happy that can find him, if
    Our grace can make him so.

Bel.　　　　I never saw
　　　　Such noble fury in so poor a thing;
　　　　Such precious deeds in one that promised nought
　　　　But beggary and poor looks.

(V.v.1–10)

Posthumus has obviously enacted his new principle effectively. He has placed his appearance and his reality under question, and the attempt to reconcile discrepancies no longer begins with the outward form but with inner valor.

The multiplicity of perspectives in the play finds expression concomitantly with the particular verbal stresses on outward and inner natures. Posthumus' awakening from his dream of ancestors and of Jupiter is the dramatic peak of his character's development, and his speech joins together these two complementary themes: the shifting perspectives through which man views the world, and the outward-inner discordancy of human nature. He awakes to find a tablet on his breast, left there by Jupiter "wherein / Our pleasure his full fortune doth confine" (V.iv.109–10).

　　　　A book? O rare one,
　　Be not, as is our fangled world, a garment
　　Nobler than that it covers. Let thy effects
　　So follow, to be most unlike our courtiers,
　　As good as promise.

But then he reads the riddle.

　　'Tis still a dream: or else such stuff as madmen
　　Tongue, and brain not: either both, or nothing,
　　Or senseless speaking, or a speaking such
　　As sense cannot untie. Be what it is,
　　The action of my life is like it, which
　　I'll keep, if but for sympathy.

(V.iv.133–51)

Posthumus' disgust stems from self-loathing, so that when he prays that the book be as noble within as its cover indicates,[9] he is speaking out of his own bitter self-recognition that he has failed to live up to his noble report. His soliloquy which opens Act V expresses his profound sense of guilt and his resolution to dedicate himself to peril, and the three scenes which lead up to his vision of familial shades and of Jupiter increase his despairing self-censure. Aware that he does not deserve reprieve, Posthumus nonetheless hopes that the vision's promise is not false, like the false courtier he has been. The riddle which the "rare book" contains does, in fact, promise his ultimate redemption, and, though he cannot decipher its conceits, he determines to allow it time to fulfill its promises. At least, he will no longer actively seek death.

The lines following his reading of the riddle reveal that Posthumus is undergoing a strenuous shift in perspective. First of all, the dream vision has brought the supernatural realm into direct contact with the natural, suggesting that, though invisible to the normal eye, the two realms may interweave more closely and more frequently than man has assumed. Posthumus suspects that his waking is a continuation of the dream, just as Imogen had suspected when she awoke from her sleeping potion ("The dream's here still" [IV.ii. 306]). If not a dream, the content of the riddle is stuff that madmen speak without reasoning about it. But Posthumus recognizes that it is "either both"—a dream merging with reality—"or nothing." The words and reason are at odds, just as the actions of Posthumus' life—being preserved in battle and now promised redemption—are at odds with reason. Because he cannot extract from evident action the causes

[9] The discrepancy between man's appearance and his true nature is often pointed by the trope of the book and its cover in Shakespeare. See, for examples, *Romeo and Juliet*, III.ii.83–84; *Pericles*, I.i.15–16, 94–95; and *Henry VIII*, I.i.122–23. In *Cymbeline*, Jupiter's book is a particularly appropriate literalization of the trope, since it occurs at the climax of a play which stresses the difference between inner nature and outward appearance.

and their effects, Posthumus accepts on faith that which he cannot rationalize. His bewildering change in perspective has suspended his ratiocinative impulses and it forces him to act out of "sympathy," which need not be defined, but only felt. Had he been true to his "sympathies" for Imogen in the first place, rather than allowing Iachimo's lies to distort the meaning of appearances, Posthumus would not have needed to learn what he now has learned through deprivation.

The limitations of human vision are under question throughout *Cymbeline*. To a certain extent, reality depends upon the person who perceives it, and habitual attitudes tend to narrow the individual's vision. In order to achieve a truer perspective of a world which cannot be contained in one fixed point of human view, it becomes necessary to look at the world from different places. Thus, Posthumus sees one reality when he looks from his place of "noble" courtier, but he sees another reality from the position of British peasant. Or again, when he assumes that Imogen is dead at his command, he sees only a man's world where consequences of action seem to be controlled by the man who directs that action. But after his dream vision that incorporates supernatural power and motive into the natural world, Posthumus can see the possibility of his actions being redeemed.

In *King Lear* (IV.vi.11–24, 69–74) Edgar creates a larger world for the blind Gloucester by convincing him that he has survived a fall from a cliff although he remains on the same spot.[10] Edgar tells him, "Thy life's a miracle" (55), a point Gloucester has been unable to "see" until he has viewed his life from more than one perspective. Edgar's speeches emphasize that reality is relative to the position from which it is viewed at the same time they stress the limitations of a

[10] Cf. Alvin Kernan, "Formalism and Realism in Elizabethan Drama: The Miracles in *King Lear*," *Renaissance Drama*, IX (1966), 59–66.

single point of view. In *Cymbeline* there are similar speeches.

When Imogen questions Pisanio about the departure of Posthumus (I.iv), she berates him for not having pressed his vision to its limits.

Imo.   Thou shouldst have made him
        As little as a crow, or less, ere left
        To after-eye him.
Pis.   Madam, so I did.
Imo. I would have broke mine eye-strings, crack'd them, but
        To look upon him, till the diminution
        Of space had pointed him sharp as my needle:
        Nay, followed him, till he had melted from
        The smallness of a gnat, to air: and then
        Have turn'd mine eye, and wept.

                            (I.iv.14–22)

Imogen tries to move beyond the limitations of the human eye in keeping the reality of Posthumus within her necessarily fixed perspective. Of course, this speech is hypothetical, since she was unable to say a proper farewell in the haste of Posthumus' departure. But her intensity, even in hypothesis, points up her sense that the reality of their love depends on their perception of it. And truly enough, when Posthumus ceases to hold his perception of Imogen's goodness and loyalty, the lapse destroys the reality of their love. In terms of the play, however, ultimate reality does not depend on man's perception of it, and his turning away does not actually diminish the nature of what remains unperceived. Thus, Imogen's goodness remains real despite the fact that Posthumus ceases to perceive it.[11] The action of his

[11] Similarly, in *The Winter's Tale*, Hermione's goodness is not actually diminished by Leontes' distorted perception of her; however, the context in which her goodness can be meaningful disappears until Leontes' vision is renewed.

life then becomes a motion toward renewed perception, toward achieving a perspective that contains more than man typically is able to see.

Belarius, too, knows the difference that the position of the human eye makes in the perception of reality. He speaks this caution to his "sons," who are unaware of their noble birth and who long for worlds they have not yet known:

> Now for our mountain sport, up to yond hill!
> Your legs are young: I'll tread these flats. Consider,
> When you above perceive me like a crow,
> That it is place which lessens and sets off,
> And you may then revolve what tales I have told you
> Of courts, of princes; of the tricks in war.
> This service is not service, so being done,
> But being so allow'd.
>
> (III.iii.10–17)

Reality depends on perception, but human vision, being limited, may not see all that there is to be seen. Certainly, this has been the case with Cymbeline's banishment of Belarius. Still, Belarius himself has tried to limit the boys' perspective to the world outside of court, giving them only his bias for perceiving that other world. The boys are aware of this, and their desire to expand their vision emphasizes the narrowness of Belarius' well-intended protection of them from the deceptions of the court world. Guiderius says,

> Out of your proof you speak: we poor unfledg'd,
> Have never wing'd from view o' th' nest; nor know not
> What air's from home. Haply this life is best
> (If quiet life be best) sweeter to you
> That have a sharper known, well corresponding
> With your stiff age; but unto us it is
> A cell of ignorance, travelling a-bed,
> A prison, or a debtor that not dares
> To stride a limit.
>
> (III.iii.27–35)

The limitations of "country" can be as narrowing for human nature as the limitations of "court." There is little doubt that extending the boundaries of both worlds is the action which the play recommends.

The imagery which Guiderius uses to express his desire for expanded vision—the vision that birds have but that man can only imagine—reiterates a pattern of images that is significant throughout the play. Of the various birds cited, the eagle supposedly has the keenest and most resilient vision, being able to look unblinkingly at the sun without damage to its eyes.[12] Imogen likens Posthumus to an eagle early in the play (I.ii.70), but the Frenchman at Philario's house warns that Posthumus' vision may be as limited as that of other men: "I have seen him in France: we had very many there could behold the sun with as firm eyes as he" (I.v. 11–13). Posthumus turns his gaze from the sun which, in the Platonic terms that seem operative here, is truth itself. But there are other eagles in the play which inform the association of Posthumus with the noble bird: Jupiter descends to the stage "sitting upon an eagle" (V.iv) and the Roman soothsayer, Philarmonus, has a vision the night before the battle in which "Jove's bird, the Roman eagle, wing'd / From the spongy south to this part of the west, / There vanish'd in the sunbeams, which portends / (Unless my sins

---

[12] See James Edmund Harting, *The Birds and Shakespeare* (London, 1871), 24, who cites various authorities on the extraordinary vision of eagles: "The opinion that the eagles possessed the power of gazing undazzled at the sun, is of great antiquity." See also Edmund Spenser's use of the idea in *The Faerie Queene* (I.x.47): "Yet wondrous quick and persant was his spright, / As Eagles eye, that can behold the Sunne." In the *Physiologus*, the eagle is a symbol of man's power to renew his vision in Christ because the bird climbed to the sun and supposedly burned off the old feathers and the dull film from his eyes (the "old man"); see *Physiologus*, trans. James Carlill, in *The Epic of the Beast* (London, n.d.), 209–10. There may be something of this tradition behind the use of the eagle in *Cymbeline*, which refers more frequently to the eagle than any other of Shakespeare's plays.

abuse my divination) / Success to th' Roman host" (IV.ii.
348–52). For a while it seems as if the soothsayer's divination has been abused, but at the conclusion of the play, the
truth of the vision returns to focus.

> The fingers of the powers above do tune
> The harmony of this peace. The vision,
> Which I made known to Lucius ere the stroke
> Of yet this scarce-cold battle, at this instant
> Is full accomplish'd. For the Roman eagle,
> From south to west on wing soaring aloft,
> Lessen'd herself and in the beams o' the sun
> So vanish'd; which foreshow'd our princely eagle,
> Th' imperial Caesar, should again unite
> His favour with the radiant Cymbeline,
> Which shines here in the west.
>
> (V.v.467–77)

More than a political harmony, the eagle's disappearance
into the sunbeams signifies as well the return of Posthumus
to the truth of Imogen's goodness. The world which his
experience of loss and renewal has revealed to him is one in
which the perspective contains the eagle's view: the earth
beneath and the heavens into which he soars.

As in *Pericles*, this wider perspective is achieved partially
through the blend of modes: tragic threats are contained to
an extent by comic presentations, and comic resolutions are
qualified by tragic impulses which remain operative. When
Iachimo tries to seduce Imogen with his lies about Posthumus' infidelity (I.vii), the threat of evil is real enough, but
his presentation of the bad report is comic. Immediately
after Imogen welcomes him, Iachimo leaps into a suddenly
intense consideration of the madness of men who cannot
distinguish between "fair and foul." Imogen is puzzled by
his abrupt soliloquy and inquires, "What makes your admiration?" Iachimo, however, seems carried away by the plea-

sure of making conceits and dwells on images of lust and depravity until Imogen can only surmise that he is ill. Realizing that he is making no progress through this oblique approach, Iachimo sends Pisanio away on a pretext and gains a more intimate audience with Imogen. She changes the subject (so she thinks) to Posthumus' health, and this gives Iachimo his cue. He proceeds to insinuate very bluntly that Posthumus has been making merry with too much boldness in Italy. Iachimo is still building his attack by circumlocution, and Imogen impatiently asks him to come to the point: "I pray you, sir, / Deliver with more openness your answers / To my demands" (87–89). Circling closer to his point, Iachimo waxes prolix with the revelation:

> Had I this cheek
> To bathe my lips upon: this hand, whose touch
> (Whose every touch) would force the feeler's soul
> To th' oath of loyalty: this object, which
> Takes prisoner the wild motion of mine eye,
> Firing it only here; should I (damn'd then)
> Slaver with lips as common as the stairs
> That mount the Capitol: join gripes, with hands
> Made hard with hourly falsehood (falsehood, as
> With labour): then by-peeping in an eye
> Base and illustrous as the smoky light
> That's fed with stinking tallow: it were fit
> That all the plagues of hell should at one time
> Encounter such revolt.
> *Imo.*   My lord, I fear,
> Has forgot Britain.
>
>   (I.vii.99–113)

Imogen's restraint in judging Posthumus from Iachimo's report reveals her emotional maturity, and her composure in the face of slander underlines Iachimo's feverish exhilaration in creating his lies. Iachimo's excitement causes him to push too far, however. When he suggests that Imogen "revenge" herself by taking him to bed, she calls out for Pisanio and denounces Iachimo severely, proudly assuring him that he is unworthy even to speak to her on the subject of Posthumus. Iachimo beats a clever retreat and admits that he was merely testing Imogen's affection, and, reversing the content of his prolixity, he eulogizes Posthumus.

Iachimo's pride in his own craftsmanship leads him beyond his goal. The evil which he is dealing in becomes subordinated by the comedy of the audience's seeing the manipulator being manipulated by the art of his craft.[13] The theatricality of the scene—in Iachimo's "feigned soliloquy"[14]—and in Imogen's melodramatic "What ho, Pisanio!" which she repeats to a servant who never appears—stresses the artifices that are conventional in seduction scenes which involve a subtle villain and a virtuous heroine. Except in melodrama, however, these conventions are not advertised, and it is interesting to note what makes this scene tragicomic rather than melodramatic.

First, the stress on artifice symbolically restates Iachimo's purpose. He, like the playwright, is working with fiction and trying to convince his audience that the fiction is real. Unlike the playwright, Iachimo is here an ineffectual artificer. Second, Imogen reveals her own human frailty in so readily accepting Iachimo's trumped-up excuse that he was testing her. She is flattered that she has passed the test and never considers his impertinence in testing her at all. She is also as flattered by his praise of Posthumus as she had been insulted by his denigrations a moment earlier. Further, she agrees to keep Iachimo's trunk in her bedchamber as an excessive gesture of apology for having suspected Iachimo at

[13] On this point and others in my general argument, cf. Arthur C. Kirsch, "*Cymbeline* and Coterie Dramaturgy," *ELH*, XXXIV (1967), 285–306.

[14] This is Edward Dowden's phrase. See Arden edition, 35 n. 32.

all. The virtuous heroine of melodrama would never show such human frailties.

The scenes in which Iachimo tries to convince Imogen and Posthumus of each other's infidelity are parallel, but the results are opposite. Because Iachimo fails to seduce Imogen, we have a momentary hope that he will also fail to pervert Posthumus' imagination. The bedchamber scene (II.ii) intervenes, however, and qualifies this comic expectation. Iachimo's admiration for Imogen's heavenly beauty briefly offsets the power of his evil intentions; at the same time, her beauty magnifies the ugliness of the "evidence" he will use to convince Posthumus. The comedy of Iachimo's failure to realize his plan contains the greatest part of his evil threat in the earlier scene, but the comedy exists conjoined to the tragic potential of the bedchamber scene. These two scenes create a tragicomic expectation—that is, opposite expectations held simultaneously—for Iachimo's approach to Posthumus (II.iv). When Posthumus succumbs, he weights the effect on the tragic side, but the ease with which he falls and the bombastic soliloquy with which he ends the scene readjust the balance. This blend of impulses, and the dramatic relationship of the comic scene to the one in which Iachimo's plan succeeds sustain the comic scene at a level more complex than melodrama.

The Queen is another advocate of evil in the play, more evil in purpose than Iachimo, and therefore excluded from the redemptive conclusion. Her plans which give the impetus to the larger actions of the play are evil in design and selfish in their ends: she wants the power of the crown to continue hers into the next generation. She apparently has Cymbeline well in control, but she wants to insure Imogen's cooperation by marrying her to Cloten. The Queen sets two of the three main plots into motion by convincing Cymbeline to advance Cloten as a suitor to Imogen and to refuse tribute to Rome; and she then functions dramatically to absorb Cymbeline's guilt. His speech on hearing of her death and of her deceptions is moving (V.v.62–68), especially when viewed under the larger construct of the inner-outward discrepancy in human nature which has deceived others in the play. Effective to purge evil from the renewed world at the play's end, the Queen demonstrates throughout the play the manner in which the threat of evil can remain operative even as it is contained in comic representation.

The anxiety which might accompany the Queen's vicious plans to poison Pisanio, and perhaps even Imogen, whom Pisanio serves, is displaced at the same moment it is created (I.vi). The physician Cornelius presents the Queen with a small box containing what she thinks are "poisonous compounds." He asks her what use she plans for them and she dissembles—a habit she has already announced (I.ii.34–37). Pisanio enters and the Queen descends upon her first prey, taking him aside while Cornelius lets the audience know that he has fooled her "with a most false effect: and I the truer, / So to be false with her" (I.vi.43–44). Her actions from this point are comic since she is unaware that her dissembling has been met with even craftier dissembling.[15]

Nonetheless the Queen's evil purposes cannot be contained only by Cornelius' deception. She shows her power again when she persuades Cymbeline to deny the tribute to Rome (III.i). This threat, even as it is being shaped in her speech, is diminished by the interruption of Cloten, who wishes to second his mother and to terminate her argument. The business of state is no doubt tedious for Cloten. Yet

[15] Granville-Barker, *Prefaces to Shakespeare*, II, 246, makes the same point and adds, "We must be interested in watching for the working out of the trick played upon her." Barbara Mowat's comments on this scene, "*Cymbeline*: Crude Dramaturgy and Aesthetic Distance," in George Walton Williams (ed.), *Renaissance Papers, 1966* (Durham, N.C., 1967), 41–43, are also similar in their conclusions.

Cymbeline's terse "Son, let your mother end" (III.i.40) injects a comic pattern which qualifies the otherwise serious matter. The Queen's speech, which out of context might be heard as an altogether commendable eulogy of Britain, is thus diminished and placed by Cloten's "second" and the king's reprimand.

The Queen's threats of evil are contained by the comic means through which she is circumvented: in these two instances by Cornelius and by Cloten. Even in her last effort, her death, she can hardly be taken too seriously because of the manner in which Cornelius reports her confession. He begins in a straightforward enough way: "With horror, madly dying, like her life, / Which (being cruel to the world) concluded / Most cruel to herself. What she confess'd / I will report, so please you" (V.v.31–34). Cymbeline encourages him to continue and the matter-of-factness of Cornelius' enumeration of her confessions is comic: "First, she confess'd she never lov'd you. . . . " The list grows so long that whatever effect of surprise might have been generated at the beginning is lost in the disproportion of the number of confessions the Queen had to make (Cornelius' report of her confession requires twenty-two lines, aside from Cymbeline's choric rejoinders). But the cap of the comedy occurs almost two hundred lines later when Imogen is accusing Pisanio of having tried to poison her. Cornelius steps forward with part of the confession he had forgot.

> O gods!
> I left out one thing which the queen confess'd,
> Which must approve thee honest. "If Pisanio
> Have," said she, "given his mistress that confection
> Which I gave him for cordial, she is serv'd
> As I would serve a rat."
>
> (V.v.243–48)

This intrusion after the matter of the Queen had been satis-
factorily completed demolishes the last shred of seriousness
which her characterization might have sustained. Like her
son Cloten's, the Queen's evil plans and even her death have
been contained in comedy.

The threat of evil is not the only effect which is offset
by comic presentation. The sense of awe engendered by
grand things—appropriate to tragedy but too overbearing
for tragicomedy—is counterbalanced as well by comic characterization. For instance, the pastoral situation of Belarius
and the two brothers in an idealized formulation would be
entirely good and polarize an entirely bad situation at court.
But the pastoral formula is no more sufficient than any other
single formula is to represent the world of Shakespeare's last
plays. Therefore Belarius has his own guilt to counterbalance
the unjustly maligned nobility of his character. He stole
Cymbeline's sons from their proper place in the world and
he has insisted on limiting their experience according to his
own necessities. His recurrent eulogies for their inherent nobility are awesome in implication but self-conscious in their
execution. The sons' retention of nobility in motive and action despite savage surroundings is an impressive fact and it
elicits admiration (especially from Imogen), but Belarius'
repetition of this point in five speeches of the last three acts
and even twice in the same scene exaggerates the situation.[16]
Excessive emphasis on the convention of princes disguised as
commoners draws the artifice itself into central focus; and
this comic stress balances the wonder of a pastoral situation
where mountaineers behave more nobly than courtiers.

The dream vision is another scene (V.iv) which inspires
a sense of awe in the characters who participate in the ad-
mirable events. But the audience is not asked to share this

[16] Belarius' speeches are the following: III.iii.79–107; IV.ii.24–30;
IV.ii.169–81; IV.iv.52–53; V.v.348–53.

sense of awe with Posthumus—or with Imogen and Belarius in the case of the noble brothers—at least not fully. Wonder is much greater in the dream vision scene because ghosts and a divinity actually appear onstage. To emphasize the spectacular quality of this wonder Jupiter even descends on an eagle. Of course, the self-consciousness of this artifice generates amazement of a sort that nullifies the wonder which a god's visitation should create within the illusion of the play. That is, the audience marvels at the mechanical strategy which lowers Jupiter to the stage more than it marvels at the descent of a god into a man's world. Aside from the mechanical ingenuity, the characterization of the god and his relationship with the ghosts displace much of the awe an audience might feel within an unbroken illusion. His first words to these suppliant shades are a reprimand.

> No more, you petty spirits of region low,
>   Offend our hearing: hush! How dare you ghosts
> Accuse the thunderer, whose bolt (you know)
>   Sky-planted, batters all rebelling coasts?
>
> (V.iv.93–96)

Jupiter's characterization is comic and he descends primarily to show how silly it is to doubt that he is controlling everything. The shades are awed and so is Posthumus, but the audience can appreciate the comic quality of these characters' previous doubt because the audience has been pushed to a distance that creates a more sensible perspective on such things. The self-conscious artifices have pointed all along to a controller of the play's incidents, and it is less of a surprise to the audience than to the characters to discover that, true enough, Jupiter has kept these "mortal accidents" under his Jovial eye with the purpose of making his gifts "the more delay'd, delighted."

The final scene is a tour de force in every critic's evaluation, and I shall not attempt to imitate those who have counted twenty-four separate denouements in it.[17] It is easier to distinguish the moments in which the tragicomic perspective shifts all these revelations into the same sphere—that inclusive container that allows the audience to see through the delightful artifices into the more profound meanings which the play has created. The resolutions progress with dramatic skill. The battle is just past, and the final scene opens with Cymbeline's praise of those who rescued him. After the report of the Queen's confession and death which holds the movement in stasis, Lucius and his train of Romans enter, catching up the gap in the dramatic progress. This forward, halting, and catch-up procedure becomes the pattern for the rest of the scene. Lucius presents Imogen-Fidele to Cymbeline and asks that the page be spared. Cymbeline becomes intrigued with the familiar features of his daughter disguised as a page and Fidele then moves into the director's position. The result of the long sequence of revelations which Imogen's inquiry about Iachimo's diamond ring sets off is the reconciliation of all domestic factions to a national harmony. Cymbeline describes it thus:

> See,
> Posthumus anchors upon Imogen;
> And she (like harmless lightning) throws her eye
> On him: her brothers, me: her master hitting
> Each object with a joy: the counterchange
> Is severally in all. Let's quit this ground,
> And smoke the temple with our sacrifices.
> [*To Belarius*] Thou art my brother; so we'll hold thee ever.
>
> (V.v.393–400)

But domestic harmony is not enough, and Imogen reminds her father about Lucius and the international problem that remains to be solved. Through Posthumus' forgiveness of

---

[17] See Nosworthy's note on p. 172 of the Arden edition.

Iachimo, Cymbeline takes his example and pardons the entire company. Posthumus then presents Jupiter's riddle and
the soothsayer interprets it according to the revelations
which have just been made. The union of the British and
the Roman nations at a level that surpasses the insularity expressed in the orginial refusal of tribute (III.i) is an expan-
sion of vision for all parties concerned. It is in large a recognition which Imogen had made in small when she was forced
to don a disguise and look for a new way of life. At that
time she had said to Pisanio:

> *Imo.*   Why, good fellow,
> What shall I do the while? Where bide? How live?
> Or in my life what comfort, when I am
> Dead to my husband?
> *Pis.*   If you'll back to th' court—
> *Imo.* No court, no father, nor no more ado
> With that harsh, noble, simple nothing,
> That Cloten, whose love-suit hath been to me
> As fearful as a siege.
> *Pis.*   If not at court,
> Then not in Britain must you bide.
> *Imo.*   Where then?
> Hath Britain all the sun that shines? Day? Night?
> Are they not but in Britain? I' th' world's volume
> Our Britain seems as of it, but not in't:
> In a great pool, a swan's nest: prithee think
> There's livers out of Britain.
>
> (III.iv.128–41)

The narrowness that fixed positions give to man's perspective has been supplanted by the eagle's overview. The
marvelous resolution of the "history" part of the play in
which both sides win fits into the larger scheme of action
in which man finds that his free choice accords with Providential design. The reunion of Britain and Rome joins traditional authority and present independence. Cymbeline freely

chooses, following Posthumus' example of forgiveness, to bring his kingdom back into harmony with a larger order.[18]

Yet *Cymbeline* is obviously more than a history play; it is a romantic comedy in which the young lovers are thwarted by parental hostility, are forced into a pastoral world where their values adjust themselves to the reality of their plight, and, through shedding of their disguises, are returned to each other under the blessing of a substantially benevolent father. But this romance has some odd quirks in its pattern. There is the "wager" plot of Iachimo, the "revenge" plot of Cloten, the "poison" plot of the Queen, the unintentional disguise of the princely brothers, not to mention the international war. The "romantic" resolutions in the final scene go awry in more than one of their typical formulations; however, all of the irregularities are logical conclusions of what the play has previously set in motion.

Aside from the counterbalancing report of the Queen's death and the enormity of her confession, the first thing that disturbs the patness of the resolution scene is the thwarting of Lucius' expectation that Imogen-Fidele will plead for his life as the favor Cymbeline has offered. Lucius generously says, "I do not bid thee beg my life, good lad, / And yet I know thou wilt." But when Imogen asks for a different "boon," Lucius is obviously surprised. The boon is Iachimo's explanation of how he happens to be wearing the ring she had given to Posthumus. Iachimo, at the center of attention, makes the most of his theatrical opportunity. He announces first that he is glad of the chance to confess and to deliver up his guilt for judgment because "a nobler sir ne'er lived / 'Twixt sky and ground" than the Posthumus

<hr />

18 William B. Thorne, "*Cymbeline*: 'Lopp'd Branches' and the Concept of Regeneration," *Shakespeare Quarterly*, XX (1969), 143–59, discusses the ritualistic aspects of the regeneration of Cymbeline through his sons with a nationalistic focus that broadens a reading of the play as "history."

he has wronged. His hyperbole of praise recalls the opening scene, in which Posthumus also received such praise—but Posthumus has traveled a vast distance between the two speeches. As Iachimo has displayed in his earlier scene of revelation with Imogen (I.vii), he is fond of rhetorical embellishment and hesitation and now he indulges in them to their limits. Cymbeline becomes impatient with him, as Imogen had earlier, and in vain asks him to "come to the matter." But Iachimo pushes his speech to the limit of prolixity, enjoying his own skill, until he sees Posthumus advancing— at which point he breaks off.

Posthumus becomes almost as involved with the art of his lamentation as Iachimo had been in the art of his revelation, and when Fidele interrupts, Posthumus resentfully strikes the page: "Shall's have a play of this? Thou scornful page, / There lie thy part." This is comic at the same time it is serious. It reveals that Posthumus has learned humility in some areas and not in others; but the astounding revelation that his action causes—the identification of Imogen—creates another "speaking such as sense cannot untie." Cymbeline cries, "Does the world go round?" and Posthumus, "How comes these staggers on me?" Reality, Posthumus discovers again, is not easy to recognize.[19] His first error had been to mistake Iachimo's lies about Imogen as truth. Now he mistakes Imogen's gesture of comfort as an attempt to upstage him. All fixed positions are made to shift their ground.

Much like Thaisa in *Pericles*, Imogen awakens from the blow in a second return to life, but she again mistakes the causes of what she sees and accuses Pisanio of treachery. The doctor steps forward and comically remembers that the Queen's confession covered this too, and things seem restored to harmony momentarily. Imogen embraces Posthu-

---

[19] As Anne Righter points out, *Shakespeare and the Idea of the Play* (London, 1964), 195.

mus but Cymbeline interrupts their enraptured gazing upon each other.

> How now, my flesh, my child?
> What, mak'st thou me a dullard in this act?
> Wilt thou not speak to me?
>
> (V.v.264–66)

Cymbeline, too, wants a part in the action of this theatrical performance. This desire, like so many of the other impulses expressed in this scene, is both comic and serious in a symbolic way. It is comic because the king must ask to be included in the party; but it is also symbolic of his passivity in the past, allowing the Queen to direct him to evil actions which have verged on destroying his kingdom's harmony. He prompts Imogen to an emotional recognition by telling her "Thy mother's dead." But when she says she is sorry, he responds, "O, she was naught." His childlikeness in wanting to matter is touching if unkinglike. The reminder nonetheless recalls the disappearance of Cloten and this leads to the discovery of Guiderius' guilt in slaying Cloten, and so on, until Cymbeline finally comments: "O rare instinct! / When shall I hear all through?" When all is finally made clear, Posthumus presents the puzzle of his riddle, and even in the deciphering of its meaning, the soothsayer includes a little comic pedantry.

> The piece of tender air, thy virtuous daughter,
> Which we call *mollis aer*; and *mollis aer*
> We term it *mulier*: which *mulier* I divine
> Is this most constant wife, who even now,
> Answering the letter of the oracle,
> Unknown to you, unsought, were clipp'd about
> With this most tender air.
>
> (V.v.447–53)

Cymbeline agrees that "this hath some seeming." Serious matters are constantly undergoing dislocation by comic perspectives which the characters cannot seem to refrain from creating by their human gestures. These gestures keep the resolution from being patent and suggest that the lesson the characters have learned may not be as fully effective as a formulaic resolution would provide. The characters have not been delivered from their human weaknesses even though they have gained new powers of vision. This retention of their human quality forces their renewed play-world to re-encounter the pressure of actuality, and this keeps the play in touch with the lives of the audience.

The complexities of *Cymbeline*'s plot and the self-consciousness with which the characters live their parts push the play beyond the limitations of conventions and formulas into a sphere where boundaries are not so well defined. The characters' growing awareness of the reality contained in illusion and the illusion involved in the actual is a microcosmic development of what the audience experiences in the same kind of recognition. Perspectives multiply bewilderingly for those who participate in life's action, but a controller of these perspectives always reminds the actor that the control is operative even when the power of reason cannot decipher its purpose. In the case of the play's audience, it is the playwright. But the powers of divinity and creativity mingle in the analogy, and the world into which the audience moves from the theater is a world which seems infused by complexities and controlling powers like those in the play they have just watched.

Chapter IV ❧ THE WINTER'S TALE
"The pleasure
of that madness"

In *The Winter's Tale*, Leontes, confronted with the breathing statue which is Hermione, pleads to keep this moment which is penultimate to actual discovery. Paulina, aware of the intensity with which Leontes has responded to the apparent statue of Hermione, offers to draw the curtain.

> *Paul.*   I'll draw the curtain:
> My lord's almost so far transported that
> He'll think anon it lives.
> *Leon.*   O sweet Paulina,
> Make me to think so twenty years together!
> No settled senses of the world can match
> The pleasure of that madness. Let 't alone.
>
> (V.iii.68–73)

Joy occurs before the factual affirmation that the world of hope and dreams coincides with the world of real experience: it occurs when the character perceives, with all his logic and rationality suspended, a tragicomic vision in which the limits of human possibility have exploded—effects no longer depend upon human causes alone.

Before Leontes can enjoy "the pleasure of that madness" which the tragicomic recognition creates, however, he must undergo the painful process of emotional growth. Like Posthumus in *Cymbeline*, Leontes achieves an inner worthiness to match his outward show only after he has endured the most difficult of adversities. Both men believe themselves responsible for the deaths of their wives because of their uncontrolled jealousy. Painful though his acknowledgment of guilt is, each accepts the responsibility for his own action, and each attempts to requite his sin by enduring—keeping his spirit alert to its own pride and acting with generosity. Leontes' penance is sixteen years longer than Posthumus', but Leontes has the added reward of a daughter's forgiveness and immediate evidence that his renewed world will continue in harmony with the next generation. Another difference is that Leontes' jealousy is completely self-inflicted; he has no qualifier of his guilt as Posthumus has in Iachimo. By omitting an outside prompter to absorb censure, Shakespeare created a different dramatic problem: How can Leontes be protected from immediate condemnation by the audience?

One of the ways in which Shakespeare meets this problem is through the character of Paulina. She and Leontes characterize each other throughout the play. Paulina plays the shrew to Leontes' tyrant in the first half of the play; in the last half, she plays confessor to Leontes' humble penitent. There are other roles through which they engage each other's nature in defining actions, but these four are primary and they control the other subsidiary roles.

Paulina's assumption of the shrewish role begins with her first appearance, which follows Leontes' public accusation of Hermione as an adulteress. Paulina's first lines to the Gaoler, under whose surveillance Hermione is imprisoned, are courtly enough; but when the Gaoler refuses to admit her to Hermione, Paulina reveals the shortness of her patience and the power of her lashing tongue (II.ii.9–12). Paulina's descent from "gentle lady" to a tough-tongued woman who calls herself "gentle" is an appropriate change for the circumstances of Leontes' court, where gentle forms have been cast aside already as a meaningful measure of gentility: Hermione's charm and graceful actions as hostess to Polixenes have been seen by the king as deceitful displays of vulgarity and lust. Although Leontes' vision is distorted by his heated imagination, he remains the source for whatever values "form" may have in his kingdom. Paulina's biting question "Is 't lawful, pray you, / To see her women? any of them? Emilia?" begins with the recognition that *law* has become a slippery term, and, in its questioning descent from "women," to "any of them," to "Emilia," it reflects how much and how swiftly the "laws" of courtesy have vanished in Leontes' court. Paulina, therefore, immediately casts herself into the role of shrew, the "scolding tongue" [1] of moral conscience in this case rather than of self-indulgent discontent. She clothes herself in the role, verbally, when Emilia informs her of the premature birth of Hermione's baby girl.

> I dare be sworn:
> These dangerous, unsafe lunes i' th' king, beshrew them!
> He must be told on't, and he shall: the office
> Becomes a woman best. I'll take 't upon me:
> If I prove honey-mouth'd, let my tongue blister,
> And never to my red-look'd anger be
> The trumpet any more.
>
> (II.ii.29–35)

Paulina's conscious assumption of her role balances Leontes' awareness of his own role-playing in his semicomic, ominous announcement: [2]

[1] Cf. *The Taming of the Shrew*, I.ii:

Renown'd in Padua for her scolding tongue.	100
I know she is an irksome brawling scold.	188
And do you tell me of a woman's tongue?	208
The one as famous for a scolding tongue.	254

[2] See S. L. Bethell's comments on the stage metaphor in this speech, *The Winter's Tale: A Study* (London, 1947), 56–57.

Go, play, boy, play: thy mother plays, and I
Play too; but so disgrac'd a part, whose issue
Will hiss me to my grave: contempt and clamour
Will be my knell. Go, play, boy, play. There have been,
(Or I am much deceiv'd) cuckolds ere now,
And many a man there is (even at this present,
Now, while I speak this) holds his wife by th' arm,
That little thinks she has been sluic'd in 's absence
And his pond fish'd by his next neighbour, by
Sir Smile, his neighbour: nay, there's comfort in't,
Whiles other men have gates, and those gates open'd,
As mine, against their will. Should all despair
That have revolted wives, the tenth of mankind
Would hang themselves.

(I.ii.187–200)

In both of these announcements of their roles, there is a comic element as well as a serious threat. Leontes' speech follows the departure of Hermione and Polixenes and climaxes his growing sense of the reality of his presumed position as cuckold. At such a moment when he sees his suspicions harden into action—the touching of hands between Hermione and Polixenes—when his suspicions seem most credible, he speaks of reality as a staged world in which the actors are playing conscious roles.[3] One psychological comfort he gains from such an effort is the sense that something larger than human choice controls each man's ability to achieve his own identity. The staged play, playing parts, implies an external controller, and being a cuckold depends more on being cast to play the part than upon a deficiency in the individual's will or personality. The responsibility of ac-

---

[3] Cf. Posthumus' emotional speech which opens Act V of *Cymbeline*, in which he also addresses the audience directly:
> You married ones,
> If each of you should take this course, how many
> Must murder wives much better than themselves
> For wrying but a little?
> (V.i.2–5)

tion and of consequences to action, therefore, Leontes rele-
gates outside himself. Such distance provides the possibility
of lessening actual pain because it removes the situation from
the world of humanly controlled action and consequence
and becomes an unavoidable set of circumstances. Thus, at
the point where Leontes' pain in recognizing what he considers to be reality becomes greater than he can bear, he shifts
his vision of it to a stage artifice which protects him from
the intensity of total involvement. He attempts to achieve
for himself the same double sense of commitment to real experience and of safety from real threat which every theater
audience knows. At the same moment that he achieves such
distance for himself, he taunts the audience with the duplicity of its position.

> There have been,
> (Or I am much deceiv'd) cuckolds ere now,
> And many a man there is (even at this present,
> Now, while I speak this) holds his wife by th' arm,
> That little thinks she has been sluic'd in 's absence.
>
> (I.ii.190–94)

Leontes moves from a character in the play, involved in the
reality of his own situation; to a perspective like the audience's, from which he surveys his role in the play; to a point
beyond the audience, from which he can show them what
they themselves are doing. These changes in points of view
are immense, and the dramatic effects they produce are complex. As any man in the audience turns to look at the woman
beside him, he realizes simultaneously that the situation is
improbable but that it is altogether possible in human terms.
In recognizing how possible Leontes' position as cuckold is,
the audience forgets for the moment that his position as
cuckold is the result of his infected fancy. There is just
enough truth in his generalization for the audience to see

that underneath his variously harsh and tyrannical attitudes, there exists (at least at given moments) a cool and rational perception of everyday realities. The surprise of the switch to the audience's personal knowledge of his situation causes laughter—the laughter of recognition that indeed this stage play is not so far-fetched as it might have seemed, or perhaps that life is not so far removed from art as it might seem. And the laughter dispels some of the horror the audience must feel at the extremities of Leontes' assumptions and the cruelties of his actions. When he says "there's comfort in't" to know that other men have experienced what he sees his own situation to be, we agree. Human frailty and the sense of humor which alone seems capable of assimilating the results of human frailty are things we know about and respect. Leontes' speech thus wins by its comic recognitions what it loses by its harsh, potentially tragic threats: the audience's sympathy. Emotional response is thereby held in a contradictory balance which forces a suspension of judgment despite Leontes' condemnable actions.

Like Leontes', Paulina's announcement of her role as shrew has comic effects as well as serious implications. When she swears to use her trumpet-tongue to tell Leontes of the danger of his delusions, she implies that she is at home in such a role: If I speak sweetly, she says, then let my tongue fail to serve me "any more." [4] The announcement of role-playing has its heroic as well as its comic heritage, but Paulina's dependence on her tongue to control situations insists on the audience's recognition of her as a shrew figure. In assuring Emilia that she will do her utmost to bring about a successful outcome of her interview with Leontes, she says:

[4] Even Paulina's tongue plays a role, as J. H. P. Pafford points out in his note to this passage, Arden edition, *The Winter's Tale*, 42 n.34-5: "The 'trumpet' was the man who preceded the herald who was usually dressed in red and often bore an angry message."

> Tell her, Emilia,
> I'll use that tongue I have.
> (II.ii.51–52)

In her interview with Leontes (II.iii), Paulina is continually characterized by his comments as a shrew, and the comic effects of this scene rely on the oldest formulas of farce. While Paulina berates him, Leontes narrows her characterization by pointing up the comic role she is enacting. The scene of the scolding shrew berating (unjustly in the formula) a poor, exhausted man is so stock that the alteration of values in this scene cannot altogether alter the evocation of sympathy for Leontes. Paulina, in defense of Hermione's goodness and the child's innocence, speaks on the side of moral right and justice, while Leontes, defending his investment in the delusion he has constructed as reality, insists on moral wrong and injustice. Yet the roles which they play as stock characters—the shrew and her weary victim—modify the force of the moral values they are enacting.

Leontes greets Paulina's entrance with both immediate anger and ironic patience:

> How!
> Away with that audacious lady! Antigonus,
> I charg'd thee that she should not come about me.
> I knew she would.
>
> (II.iii.41–44)

This formulaic response to a stock situation creates an amusing and ironic distance between Leontes and the trial he is undergoing. The scene begins by establishing itself as a comic routine and it continues to follow the pattern. Antigonus protests that he tried to stop her with threats of Leontes' displeasure and his own, but obviously with no effect. Leontes' sarcastic response insures Paulina's shrewish characterization: "What! canst not rule her?" In her re-

sponse, she agrees to the role: " . . . in this—. . . trust it, /
He shall not rule me" (47, 49–50). Throughout the scene
Leontes counters Paulina's accusations with accusations
about her role as shrew, each time increasing the farcical
effect and displacing his formulaically sympathetic position
in the comic routine.

> Thou dotard! thou art woman-tir'd, unroosted
> By thy dame Partlet here.
>
> (II.iii.74–75)

> He dreads his wife.
>
> (79)

> A callat
> Of boundless tongue, who late hath beat her husband,
> And now baits me! [5]
>
> (90–92)

> A gross hag!
> And, lozel, thou art worthy to be hang'd,
> That wilt not stay her tongue.
>
> (107–109)

Leontes' chief means of projecting Paulina's image is, of
course, through reference to her husband, Antigonus. Leontes works upon Antigonus' sense of pride and manly dignity in order to force him to banish Paulina, but Antigonus
reacts with equanimity. He answers the accusation that he
cannot stay his wife's tongue with a comic appeal to the
universality of his situation.

> Hang all the husbands
> That cannot do that feat, you'll leave yourself
> Hardly one subject.
>
> (II.iii.109–11)

---

[5] Bethell, *The Winter's Tale*, 60, comments that "the pun ('beat',
'bait') suggests a further note of comedy."

Antigonus' joke echoes Leontes' earlier remark that a tenth of mankind might hang themselves for cuckolds (I.ii.200), and it has the same effect of comic displacement in a tragically threatening situation.[6]

The stock situation diametrically opposes the narrative situation, and the complexity of emotional responses produced by the opposition is significant in several ways. It is necessary to achieve some sympathy for Leontes in order to prepare him a place in the comic resolution of the play; his guilty action must be capable of redemption. He is a self-crossed figure and the soliloquy which precedes Paulina's entrance reveals him pathetically caught in the consequences of his own erroneous action. His torment, although it causes him to contemplate the further horror of murdering Hermione to ease his pain, does for a brief moment evoke pity. Paulina's entrance at such a moment, when Leontes is most distracted by news of his son's illness and by paranoiac thoughts of having become a joke to Camillo and Polixenes, increases the possibility of compassion for Leontes. Verbal flagellation at such a time could hardly be accepted by anyone. Yet the comic distance achieved through establishing the characters in their stock positions—Paulina as a shrew, Antigonus as her hen-pecked and ineffectual husband, and Leontes as the long-suffering victim of her tongue—works both to remove Paulina from a wholly commendable position and also to dispel the pathos of Leontes' grappling with his sorrow.

Without the qualification of the stock characterization, the audience would naturally respond favorably toward the moral justice of Paulina's position and it would as unre-

---

[6] Antigonus' presence in this scene acts as yet another buffer for Leontes, absorbing some of Paulina's harshness. Caught between the vitriolic accusations of both Paulina and Leontes, Antigonus' comic dilemma both mitigates and protects the seriousness of his wife and his king.

servedly admire her honesty and psychological insights into Leontes' self-delusions. Consistently, the audience would readily condemn Leontes for his jealousy and violence toward the gentle Hermione. Yet Shakespeare has offset these natural propensities by his use of stock comic characterization. The conflict between moral evaluation and emotional sympathy requires a hesitation of commitment on the part of the audience, and the conflict delays judgment until the revelation of Apollo's oracle, which is the climax of emotional tension in the first part of the play.

After the revelation of Apollo's oracle and Hermione's apparent death, Leontes' reliance upon Paulina is in one sense a replacement or compensation for the loyalty he had owed Hermione and which he had held from her. Immediately after the announcement of Mamillius' death, Hermione faints, and Paulina collects the overcharged and scattered emotional atmosphere into a single awesome focus:

> This news is mortal to the queen: look down
> And see what death is doing.
>
> (III.ii.148-49)

Her directive becomes the "still center" of the scene and, in a larger view, of the entire action of the play. The final resurrection of Hermione depends upon the conviction that Paulina's interpretation of Hermione's swoon carries. Leontes tries to modify the fatality of Paulina's reading—"Her heart is but o'ercharged: she will recover"—but Paulina's calm and direct evaluation cannot be so easily resisted. In her two powerful lines, Paulina has changed her position from subject of Leontes to ruler. But even as she moves into her new role in relationship to Leontes, her harshness absorbs the censurable effects of his guilty action. While she is gone to attend Hermione, Leontes admits his sin and begins to plan how he will amend it (155–56). Paulina rushes back and for twenty-five lines torments him with tongue-lashing accusations, delaying the revelation that the queen is dead. Then she invites Leontes to "despair" rather than to repent and repair his soul, and Leontes brokenly submits to the justness of even this.

> Go on, go on:
> Thou canst not speak too much; I have deserv'd
> All tongues to talk their bitt'rest.
>
> (III.ii.214–16)

In submitting to the shrew, Leontes makes partial amends for his previous tyranny. Paulina's fury does not abate easily, however, and she extends her verbal punishment of Leontes beyond humane limits (218–32). Her intense and bitter accusations produce another important effect aside from absorbing part of the hostility that Leontes' actions have generated: they convince the audience that Hermione is, in fact, dead.

The scene ends with Leontes asking Paulina to lead him to his sorrows. When the play's action again returns to Sicilia (V.i), it is immediately evident that Leontes has allowed Paulina emotional dictatorship over him, and that for sixteen years she has been his priestess and confessor. Cleomenes attempts to soothe Leontes' guilt and sorrow, but Paulina still needles him to confess his sin.

> Cleo. Sir, you have done enough, and have perform'd
> A saint-like sorrow: . . .
> Do as the heavens have done, forget your evil;
> With them, forgive yourself.
> Leon.   Whilst I remember
> Her, and her virtues, I cannot forget
> My blemishes in them. . . .
> Paul.   True, too true, my lord:
> If, one by one, you wedded all the world,
> Or from the all that are took something good,

> To make a perfect woman, she you kill'd
> Would be unparallel'd.
> *Leon.*   I think so. Kill'd!
> She I kill'd! I did so: but thou strik'st me
> Sorely, to say I did: it is as bitter
> Upon thy tongue as in my thought. Now, good
>   now,
> Say so but seldom.
> *Cleo.*   Not at all, good lady:
> You might have spoken a thousand things that
>   would
> Have done the time more benefit and grac'd
> Your kindness better.
>   (V.i.1–23)

Despite the essential change in their relationship, Paulina still enjoys the power of her shrewish tongue. The concern is now whether Leontes should marry again. Most of his subjects want an heir and would encourage his remarriage, but Paulina exacts Leontes' promise "Never to marry, but by my free leave. . . . Unless another / As like Hermione as is her picture, / Affront his eye" (V.i.70, 73–75). When Cleomenes tries to stop her bargaining with the king, she says, true to the prolixity of her stock characterization,

>   I have done.
> Yet, if my lord will marry,—if you will, sir;
> No remedy but you will,—give me the office
> To choose you a queen: she shall not be so young
> As was your former, but she shall be such
> As, walk'd your first queen's ghost, it should take joy
> To see her in your arms.[7]
>   (V.i.75–80)

---

[7] There is a submerged insistence in this speech and in others which Paulina makes in this scene that Hermione remains, even in death, a vital figure. This is one of the subtle ways by which the audience is prepared, against its "factual" knowledge, for the ultimate revelation that Hermione lives.

She has forced Leontes to allow her yet another role with which to rule him—now she is his procuress. When Perdita and Florizel petition Leontes to be their advocate before Polixenes, and Leontes seems to admire Perdita's beauty a little too much, Paulina quickly reminds him of their contract.

> Sir, my liege,
> Your eye hath too much youth in 't; not a month
> 'Fore your queen died, she was more worth such gazes
> Than what you look on now.
>
> (V.i.223–26)

Leontes assures her that he was thinking of Hermione in admiring Perdita, but at this point only the audience knows how justified he is to do so.[8]

The comic pattern of Paulina's and Leontes' relationship continues into the final scene, where the living Hermione is revealed. Paulina forces Leontes into an intensely emotional state of anticipation and then threatens to draw the curtain upon the statue. Through her threats to close off the revelation, however, she builds the kind of imaginative excitement that the tragicomic recognition requires. By threats of frustration, she dispels rational skepticism that would "hoot" at the revelation of the living Hermione "like an old tale." She achieves, with the confident skill of a good stage director, or a good playwright, the fusion of illusion and reality into joyful truth.

---

8 In *Pericles* and *Cymbeline* also the father finds the "unknown" features of his daughter not only familiar, but love-inspiring. Finding one's own image renewed in youth and innocence regenerates the father in each case, although he is at a loss to explain the cause. Despite the similarities of these scenes in each play, each father-daughter recognition receives different dramatic handling. In *Pericles*, it is the climactic moment in the play. In *Cymbeline*, Imogen is disguised as a boy when her familiar features move her father to love. Leontes' admiration of Perdita ironically complies with Paulina's prescription that a new wife should closely resemble Hermione. Paulina, of course, quickly emphasizes her other stricture, "she shall not be so young / As was your former" (V.i.78–79), when she reminds Leontes that his "eye hath too much youth in 't."

The discovery of that joyful truth is so exhilarating that no one worries about the trickery involved in creating it. The experience of wonder justifies the artifices used to make that experience possible. The "voice of moral justice" has deceived not only Leontes, but the audience as well. We experience, as he does, "the pleasure of that madness" which "no settled senses of the world can match." And the experience is so delightful that we can forgive a little skillful trickery along the way. If, upon leaving the theater, we are at ease to ponder the significance of that trickery, we confront once again that profound dislocation of fixed perceptions which Shakespeare's tragicomedy produces. There are more realities than meet the eye in these final plays. Or, to put it more precisely, the eye is trained to look through the artifice into a world of wonder.

The tragicomic resolution in *The Winter's Tale* can be as powerful as it is because of other balances which also operate throughout the play. The structural division in time has often led critics mistakenly to assume that Acts IV and V are the comic performance of the tragic action of the first three acts. Each part has a dominant impulse, it is true, but that impulse is consistently balanced throughout. The tragicomic blend created in the first half, in large part by the pairing of Leontes and Paulina, is sustained in the last half by similar means: that is, by balancing Autolycus against the pastoral figures, the Shepherd and the Clown. In Leontes' court, complexities and hyperboles build to a dramatic inflation, which Apollo's direct and terse oracle punctures. In the less sophisticated world of Bohemia, however, there is an inverse need for complexity and duplicity. Autolycus, as a kind of "fallen" Apollo,[9] a peddler of ballads, provides a

---

[9] Autolycus' classical lineage to which he refers (IV.iii.24–26) is found in Ovid's *Metamorphoses*, XI.298–317 (and in Homer's *Odyssey*, XIX). As he says, Autolycus was "littered under Mercury," but Apollo

decadent complexity to balance the pastoral simplicity of the last acts of the play.

Autolycus' complexity manifests itself most directly in his disguises. He is a Protean figure who seems to be undergoing a continuous metamorphosis, at least in his relationships with the other characters in the play. On his first appearance he announces his identity and his past connection with Prince Florizel between snatches of song (IV.iii.13–14, 23–30). His self-conscious announcement of his role is a parodic reminder of Paulina's and Leontes' previous announcements as well as a preparation for Perdita's and Florizel's descriptions of their own disguised roles (IV.iv.1–35). Autolycus' first disguise is involved with the parodic enactment of the Good Samaritan story.[10] The parody itself calls attention to the artifice of disguise—Autolycus is hardly the victim of the scene. But even more emphatic of the artifice is the fact that Autolycus is disguised as his own victim. The double humor which results from his self-description is similar to that which Falstaff creates in his speech when, playing the role of Prince Hal, he praises "valiant Jack Falstaff" (*1 Henry IV*, II.iv.512–27). Autolycus says of his oppressor,

> A fellow, sir, that I have known to go about with troll-my-dames: I knew him once a servant of the prince: I cannot tell, good sir, for which of his virtues it was, but he was certainly whipped out of the court.
>
> (IV.iii.84–87)

The Clown's literal sensibility causes him to quibble over Autolycus' choice of words—"His vices, you would say;

---

was also involved. According to Ovid, both Apollo and Mercury wanted Chione, Autolycus' mother, but Apollo waited to approach her until evening, according to his sense of decorum, while Mercury seduced her in the afternoon. Chione's offspring, fraternal twins, were Philammon by Apollo and Autolycus by Mercury. Shakespeare's Autolycus seems to embody characteristics of both twins, in his singing and in his thieving.

[10] This parody has been noted by several critics; but see G. Wilson Knight, *The Crown of Life* (London, 1965), 101.

there's no virtue whipped out of the court" (IV.iii.88). The Clown ignores the other meanings of "virtue" (power, and the skill of manipulation) and the point makes clear the vast difference between pastoral simplicity and Autolycus' sophisticated multiplicity. The pun and the metaphor (like disguise) are his tools and with them Autolycus transforms life into an artifice which he sells back to the Clown on a literal level.

When Autolycus appears again, for example, he is once more disguised: under a false beard, he peddles his ballads. The servant announces him with great enthusiasm—Autolycus' repertoire is endless—and his entrance enhances the festive mood of the scene. Like Shrove Tuesday, Autolycus brings release from mundane realities. And, in the same way that Carnival acts as an exorciser of evil spirits, the sheep-shearing celebration purges the play of its melancholy. There is a self-conscious pointing to the nature of art and its relationship to life in both farcical action and serious debate in this scene. Mopsa and Dorcas enact on a farcical level the audience's desire for artistic illusions. Their reiterated questions about the "truth" of the ballads corresponds to the audience's demands for realism in art. Autolycus' responses, like those of the expert artificer he imitates, are equivocal:

> *Mop.* Is it true, think you?
> *Aut.* Very true, and but a month old. . . .
> Why should I carry lies abroad?
> (IV.iv.267–72)

As is so often the case in comedy, the rhetorical question does not contain its own answer. The reason for carrying lies abroad, at the level of Autolycus' thieving instincts, is to gain a "prize" from those who are gullible enough to accept his lies as truth. At the analogous level of audience and playwright, the motive is much the same. There is a demand, a need, in the life of man to experience poetic lies, and the playwright satisfies this need. Drama is not so different from the confidence man's art that Autolycus practices.[11] Success in both requires a remarkable understanding of and sympathy with human needs. That is one of the reasons that Autolycus, like Falstaff, is such a well-loved rogue. He understands human weaknesses and he does not condemn them.[12]

Everyone at the sheep-shearing festival is disguised except for the Shepherd and the Clown, and the abundance of disguise in this simple pastoral setting calls attention to the dislocation of identities in the idyllic world. Polixenes soon explodes the artifice by demanding that Florizel return to his proper role as Prince and give over his illusions about being a rustic lover (IV.iv.418–42); but disguise remains the means to discovery. Camillo advises Florizel to exchange garments with Autolycus and to flee to Sicilia. At this point, both Autolycus and Florizel wear their former disguises: Autolycus is the bearded peddler and Florizel is like "Golden Apollo, a poor humble swain" (IV.iv.30). When Autolycus exchanges clothes with Florizel, he is assuming Florizel's pastoral disguise, which he then flaunts to the Shepherd and Clown as a courtier's garments. This excessive complexity in which one disguise cancels another insists on the artificiality of the convention and points out its logical absurdities. At the same time it reiterates the Autolycus-Apollo parodic analogy and reminds us that Autolycus is a corrupt version of the dramatic force that Apollo manifests in the first half of the play. Autolycus' riddles are not oracles but ballads; yet both affirm their audience's need for assurance that truth may be found within the poetic lie.

The tragicomic balance of contradictory impulses mani-

---

11 Cf. Bethell's comments on Autolycus, *The Winter's Tale*, 46.

12 In contrast, Perdita displays a stern resistance to artificiality in her famous debate with Polixenes on the relationship of art and nature. See IV.iv.79–103.

fests itself in aspects other than characterization. For example, the opening scene establishes the pattern of oppositions by creating an atmosphere of excess, which is dotted throughout with ironies. Archidamus' first remark is weighted with dramatic irony, as are most of the evaluations in this scene. He says that Sicilia's hospitality will be difficult to match—Bohemia is apparently a less magnificent land (I.i.1–4, 11–16). Unwittingly, Archidamus has labeled the problem: Leontes' and Polixenes' worlds differ. The rarity of Sicilian magnificence has intoxicated even the language of common conversation.[13] Both Archidamus and Camillo speak with courtly exaggeration which contrasts sharply with the simpler expressions of Bohemia's Shepherd (III.iii.59 ff.). But Camillo's caution, that Archidamus' praise of Sicilia and fear of Bohemia's insufficiency is too great, is couched in a vocabulary that becomes symbolically significant in the following action—not only Archidamus pays "a great deal too dear" for Sicilia's "free gifts," but so do Polixenes, Hermione, and even Camillo. The vocabulary of trade, introduced so early in an innocent way, builds gradually to an ominous significance in the barter of souls Leontes conducts in the trial scene. Hermione recognizes Leontes' superior power as tradesman, but she verbally steps beyond the marketplace.

> Sir,
> You speak a language that I understand not:
> My life stands in the level of your dreams,
> Which I'll lay down. . . .
>   Sir, spare your threats:
> The bug which you would fright me with, I seek.
> To me can life be no commodity.
>
>   (III.ii.79–82, 91–93)

[13] See Mary L. Livingston's discussion of the dangerous effects of exaggerated language in "The Natural Art of *The Winter's Tale*," *Modern Language Quarterly*, XXX (1969), 340–55.

At this moment of withdrawal, Hermione recognizes the impossibility of existing in a world where the metaphor and its literal correlative have been severed. No longer is she the graciously insistent hostess ("Will you go yet? / Force me to keep you as a prisoner, / Not like a guest: so you shall pay your fees / When you depart, and save your thanks?" [I.ii.51–54]), nor the secure wife who expects to hear compliments from her husband ("Our praises are our wages" [I. ii.94]). Hermione understands only that Leontes has imagined an illicit bargain between her and Polixenes. Unable to combat a vision which she cannot see, she places her life at Leontes' disposal since the terms which made it valuable no longer exist. The way in which she detaches herself from her life, by viewing it as a "commodity," creates the possibility and the meaning of her sixteen-year retreat. Until the values which make her life a true commodity can be had, she moves beyond the realm of Leontes' marketplace, where life exists only in metaphor.

The vocabulary of trade is a rhetorical figure, a terrible metaphor, in the world of Leontes' mad vision, but in Bohemia it becomes a literal reality (IV.iii.36 ff.). The transition from metaphor to literality signifies the general movement of the play. Autolycus' "hot brain" (IV.iv.684) parodies Leontes' heated imagination, but with a significant difference: Autolycus' imagination does not labor over moral constructs, but only over practical matters like robbing a purse.[14] The literal application of the terms of trade to the actual marketplace, whether it be the rogue's road

[14] Pafford, Arden edition, lxxx, says that Autolycus "serves as a faint rhythmic parallel to the evil of Leontes in the first part of the play." Autolycus is also a parodic figure who links the Leontes of the first half of the play to the Leontes of the last act. Autolycus has changed garments with Florizel, and he tells the Shepherd and the Clown of the punishment in store for them at the hands of Polixenes. They hire him to be their advocate to the king (IV.iv.808–809). In the very next scene, Florizel asks Leontes to be his advocate to Polixenes (V.i.220).

or the produce stalls, is an appropriate use of language. But the application of such terms to human life and acts of faith signifies a breach in decorum that reaches metaphysical proportions. The rest of the play's action attempts to bring the metaphor back into an appropriate relationship with actuality.

Similarly, Camillo's speech about the common boyhood of the two kings (I.i.21–32) suggests a metaphorical perfection which life's actions cannot match. The garden of innocence inevitably gives way to knowledge, but no one in Sicilia seems to comprehend the pattern.[15] The wisdom comes in understanding how to relate the adult world of knowledge to the child's world of innocence. Leontes seems to have leapt from one to the other without any mediation. He therefore tries to match the extreme of the one—absolute innocence—with the extreme of the other—absorption in the knowledge of evil. His directive to Mamillius to "go play" and his supposition that Hermione "plays" voice these extremes (I.ii.187).[16] The expectations of Archidamus and Camillo in the opening scene express the same kind of unrealistic naiveté about the human spirit. When Camillo asks that "the heavens continue their loves," Archidamus responds, "I think there is not in the world either malice or matter to alter it" (I.i.31–34). Maintaining the absolute in human love is an expectation based upon tenuous ideals. That the expectation is not attached to actuality is immediately proved by Leontes' jealousy, and the enlightening process which all the characters undergo for the rest of the

---

[15] The pastoral innocence of Bohemia likewise succumbs to knowledge when Polixenes demands that his son divorce himself from his illusions.

[16] M. M. Mahood, *Shakespeare's Wordplay* (London, 1957), 153–55, makes some interesting suggestions about Leontes' speech, especially concerning his failure to "recapture the non-moral vision of childhood" in which "play" can refresh. Leontes' "bawdy use of play," Miss Mahood says, "suggests the moral rigidity born of a moral uncertainty."

play aims toward reuniting the metaphor and the actual world which it represents.

One of the most important scenes in the first part of the play, which functions as a standard of true values against which the whole of Leontes' mad world is ironically placed, involves the return of Cleomenes and Dion from Delphos (III.i). Cleomenes opens the scene describing the "delicate climate" and "sweet air" of Apollo's isle. The degree to which he has been impressed suggests an implicit contrast to what he has been accustomed to in Sicilia: Leontes' accusations burden the air of his isle. Dion praises the ceremony of sacrifice they have witnessed at Delphos. Again the contrast is implicit. The audience has just witnessed the sacrifice of Hermione's daughter to banishment and probable death (II.iii.172–82). But Leontes' sacrifice of the babe was conducted feverishly, abruptly, and without ceremony in contrast to Dion's description: "O, the sacrifice! / How ceremonious, solemn and unearthly / It was i' th' offering!" (III. i.6–8). The implicit contrast points up the fact that Leontes has assumed the position of a god, to whom sacrifices must be made in truncated and hubristic ceremonies. Not only has Leontes sacrificed Perdita to the elements in the scene preceding this one; in the scene which follows he sacrifices Hermione as well. In so doing, he denies Apollo's superior power—"There is no truth at all i' th' Oracle" (III.ii.140)— and earns the punishment of his son's death. Leontes, like Cleomenes, is reduced to "nothing" by the "voice o' th' Oracle." In the scene of Cleomenes and Dion's report, hyperbole is appropriately used to describe the god. This example of proper use exposes the dangerous excess of hyperbole in Leontes' world. Man is an inappropriate object for absolute praise, and through ironic contrast, this scene prepares for the deflation of Leontes' "dream" which the oracle effects. In this scene, hyperbole becomes the simple equivalent of truth, a paradox which serves as a fulcrum for the unbalanced judgments in the scenes on either side of it.

The return from Delphos also provides a bridge that compresses the time between Leontes' accusation of Hermione and her trial. A spatial, or geographical, bridge occurs in the scene which shows Antigonus depositing Perdita on the coast of Bohemia.[17] In addition to this function, the scene achieves one of the clearest balances of contradictory impulses in the play. Many critics seem unwilling to accept the blend of tragic and comic effects of Antigonus' famous "exit," however, and they insist that the action be read as either one or the other.[18] The stage direction itself is simple and straightforward after slight preparation in Antigonus' lines.

> A savage clamour!
> Well may I get aboard! This is the chase:
> I am gone for ever!   *Exit, pursued by a bear.*
> (III.iii.55–58)

Antigonus obviously hears the bear roar—either offstage or immediately after the bear enters—and in the space of half a line he himself is running off the stage, probably flinging his last line over his shoulder as he runs. Speed is part of the

---

[17] Shakespeare's use of a "coast" for inland Bohemia is a long-standing topic for critical debate. I question Pafford's assertion, Arden edition, 66 n. 2, that "the explanation surely is that Shakespeare was simply following *Pandosto* which mentions the coast of Bohemia." In a play where other anomalies and anachronisms figure so clearly in the methods of self-conscious artistry, surely this error has a similar effect of drawing the audience's attention to a "fact" which is "fiction."

[18] Critics who emphasize the "serious" reading of the scene usually stress the symbolic meaning of the bear. See Knight, *The Crown of Life*, 98; Dennis Biggins, "'Exit pursued by a Beare': A Problem in *The Winter's Tale*," *Shakespeare Quarterly*, XIII (1962), 3–13; and Pafford, Arden edition, lix, 69. For the comic reading, see E. M. W. Tillyard, *Shakespeare's Last Plays* (London, 1938), 77–78; Bethell, *The Winter's Tale*, 64–65; and Nevill Coghill, "Six Points of Stage-Craft in *The Winter's Tale*," *Shakespeare Survey*, XI (1958), 34–35.

tragicomic effect. The surprise of the bear's appearance and the quick shift in Antigonus' prospects from life to death are the points which cause laughter, and prolonging the action between Antigonus and the bear, as some critics would do,[19] violates the effect. If the scene is exploited in either direction, the audience will have too much time to reflect on the meaning of the action.[20] If the scene is played quickly, the immediate appearance of the Shepherd, who finds Perdita, and of the Clown, who describes in such a comic way the shipwreck and the sounds of the bear's dining on Antigonus, dictate the response the audience must make to the event. Shakespeare leaves little to chance, carefully directing audience response into the appropriate channel.

Perdita's safety is assured, and that releases anxiety about her fate. The Shepherd's speculation that "this has been some stair-work, some trunk-work, some behind-door-work" (III.iii.73–75) places Leontes' jealous suspicions into their proper proportions. Whereas the suspicion of infidelity is a tragic problem to Leontes and to Antigonus (II.i.140–50; III.iii.41–53), it becomes a comic commonplace in the speech of the Shepherd. The extremes balance each other and delay the need to have the matter settled. The Shepherd's comment creates an emotional balance which allows the action to continue in its tragicomic way. The Clown's narrative of

[19] Coghill, "Six Points of Stage-Craft," 34, suggests that a "well-timed knock-about routine" is "needed" between Antigonus and the bear. Biggins, "A Problem in *The Winter's Tale*," 12–13, errs in the opposite direction by trying to give a graceful dignity to one of the clumsiest of creatures: the child "could naturally be supposed to lie motionless, thus lending plausibility at once to the 'child' and to the 'bear's' actions in treating it with respect, the animal perhaps sniffing gently at it before pursuing Antigonus off the stage."

[20] I am not suggesting that the symbolic force of the bear as an emblem of wrath does not operate in this scene. But the audience is not given time to ponder intricate symbolic relationships; the response is automatic rather than contemplative. For the tradition of the bear as an emblem of wrath, see Lawrence J. Ross, "Shakespeare's 'Dull Clown' and Symbolic Music," *Shakespeare Quarterly*, XVII (1966), 126.

the storm at sea, which swallows the ship, and of the bear's swallowing Antigonus on land competes with the Shepherd's attempt to tell how he found Perdita. Each has a miraculous adventure to tell, and each is comically eager to impress the other with his experience.[21] The Clown wins first chance, and his conscientious attempt to balance each of his "two sights" suggests his pride in his narrative skill. The exactitude of the parallel diminishes the seriousness of both events—they seem to exist in order to point up the artifice of analogous structure. The Shepherd's response to his son's story is as artificial as the story itself.

> *Shep.* Would I had been by, to have helped the old man!
> *Clo.*　I would you had been by the ship side, to have helped
> 　　　her: there your charity would have lacked footing.
> 　　　　　　　　　　　　　　　　　　　(III.iii.106–10)

The Clown is well aware of the difference between good intentions and good actions. The Shepherd, however, wins the storytelling contest by his felicitous use of symbolism. There is a self-consciousness in his voicing of it—"Now bless thyself: thou met'st with things dying, I with things new-born" —that reinforces the sense of contest in narrative skill.[22] But the Clown's response when they discover the gold is a comic deflation of any symbolic pretenses the Shepherd may have had: "You're a made old man: if the sins of your youth are forgiven you, you're well to live. Gold! all gold!" (119–20). The Shepherd's cupidinous instinct is as keen as his son's, and he is in a hurry to hide the gold in hopes that it will multiply: "This is fairy gold, boy, and 'twill prove so; up

---

[21] It is possible that Shakespeare was creating a conscious parody here of the traditional singing matches between shepherds in the pastoral eclogues.

[22] Bethell, *The Winter's Tale*, 66, 89, perhaps overstresses the religious symbolism in these lines. Although he is generally cognizant of the mixture of tragic and comic impulses, he does not notice the possibility of a comic effect from the self-consciousness in these lines.

with 't, keep it close: home, home, the next way. We are lucky, boy; and to be so still requires nothing but secrecy. Let my sheep go: come, good boy, the next way home" (III.iii.121–25). His urgency to get home and hide his treasure overrides his former concern for his strayed sheep and the line "Let my sheep go" insists on the parodic effect of the entire episode. This Shepherd is no saint; given a choice between duty and gold, he knows which to follow. The Clown, too, expresses more curiosity than compassion for Antigonus: "I'll go see if the bear be gone from the gentleman, and how much he hath eaten" (127–28).

These rustics have a healthy manner of accepting the ways of the world that contrasts sharply with the over-idealizations which characterized Sicilia. They are not pastoral examples of virtue, nor do we want them to be. The battle between virtue and vice in Leontes' court has been strenuous. Through the eyes of the Clown we see Antigonus as a stranger, and the distance that the Clown's impersonal perspective gains releases the audience from their sympathetic investment in Antigonus. Antigonus' death, thus, becomes impersonalized both through the artifice of the bear and through the Clown's narrative manner. In the same way, through the Shepherd's response to Perdita, the world of Leontes' infected imagination becomes remote. The new world momentarily seems closer to us than Sicilia, but lest we become too familiar with its people, Time steps out upon the stage to remind us to keep our distance: the stage is the stage, the play is the play, and we are the audience.[23]

Moving in and out of the illusion is an important part of the tragicomic progress toward an ultimate recognition which requires ambivalent vision. We enter the action at the same time we retain a safe distance from its consequences.

[23] Cf. Bethell's discussion, *ibid.*, 52–55, of the deliberate emphasis on the duality of the play world and the real world.

Yet, every time we "lose" ourselves in the play, Shakespeare calls our attention to what we have done. He forces us to look at our yearning for imaginative experience and to evaluate that yearning.

The last two scenes of *The Winter's Tale* even define the effect which Shakespeare's tragicomic mode aims toward, as if Shakespeare wanted to insure the audience's awareness of what they are experiencing as they experience it. Autolycus has missed the meeting of the two kings and he asks a gentleman for the story.

> *First Gent.* I make a broken delivery of the business; but the changes I perceived in the king and Camillo were very notes of admiration: they seemed almost, with staring on one another, to tear the cases of their eyes: there was speech in their dumbness, language in their very gesture; they looked as they had heard of a world ransomed, or one destroyed: a notable passion of wonder appeared in them; but the wisest beholder, that knew no more but seeing, could not say if th' importance were joy or sorrow; but in the extremity of the one it must needs be.
>
> (V.ii.9–19)

This definition of "wonder" seems as critically self-conscious as the famous debate between Perdita and Polixenes on nature and art in the sheep-shearing scene (IV.iv.86–103). As Harold S. Wilson points out, the use of horticultural illustrations was familiar in discussions of nature and art in the Renaissance and earlier, and the subject itself had long been a critical commonplace.[24] Critical concern with the definition and use of "wonder" or *admiratio* was likewise commonplace.[25] The unusual things about both of these

[24] Harold S. Wilson, " 'Nature and Art' in *Winter's Tale*, IV.iv.86 ff.," *Shakespeare Association Bulletin*, XVIII (1943), 114–20.
[25] See Marvin T. Herrick, "Some Neglected Sources of *Admiratio*,"

passages are not their content, but their self-consciousness and dramatic appropriateness. The first quality is part of Shakespeare's attempt to weave the illusory and the actual into an ambivalent consciousness in the audience. The second, dramatic appropriateness, is also a conscious pleasure, based on the intellectual perception of irony.

In the sheep-shearing festival many ironies add to the pleasure of our perception of the scene as a whole. Two major ones are the fact that almost everyone at the party is disguised, and the fact that part of the scene's structure resembles the masque, a sophisticated court entertainment.[26] The pastoral world seems to have at least as much sophistication in form as the court, despite the simpler, more basic experiences it celebrates. The debate on nature and art comes appropriately into the focus of a scene which observes natural seasons in artificial forms. The irony which Polixenes himself enacts is more obvious, however. He says,

> You see, sweet maid, we marry
> A gentler scion to the wildest stock,
> And make conceive a bark of baser kind
> By bud of nobler race. This is an art
> Which does mend nature—change it rather—but
> The art itself is nature.
>
> (IV.iv.92–97)

Not long after, he condemns this very practice where his own son is concerned (IV.iv.418–42). The discrepancy between what he says and what he does—the difference between theory and action—is comic and relieves the tension that his threats to the young lovers create. Further irony exists, of course, in the discrepancy between Perdita's actual

MLN, LXII (1947), 222–26; and J. V. Cunningham, *Woe or Wonder: The Emotional Effect of Shakespearean Tragedy* (Denver, 1951), 22–23.

26 For some interesting comments on the use of the masque in this scene, see J. M. Nosworthy, "Music and Its Function in the Romances of Shakespeare," *Shakespeare Survey*, XI (1958), 67.

heritage and her pastoral identity. Her insistence on keeping the stock pure is the theory which Polixenes' action supports and which the final revelation of the play defends. The liberality of Polixenes' speech, despite its ironic placement of his own actions, opens an avenue of critical awareness that qualifies somewhat the formulaically decorous matching of persons in the conclusion.

The qualification of the final scene takes place beforehand, however, so that its power is greater. All possible reservations are displaced before the reunion of Leontes and Hermione so that the pure wonder of their joy may be experienced without reservation. It is in this way that the scene of the gentlemen's report of the kings' meeting functions. Each gentleman has caught only a part of the meeting, and each gives a stylistically distinct narration: the First and Second Gentlemen relate with as little embellishment as possible the wonder of each event they saw, and the Third Gentleman elaborates, with grand hyperboles, the rest of the action (V.ii.9–91). The tripartite narrative recalls the part-song of Autolycus, Mopsa, and Dorcas (IV.iv.298–307), and the Second Gentleman, Rogero, emphasizes that the ballad-makers could not express the wonder of the moment, a point underlined by Autolycus' silent presence throughout this scene. The gentlemen's narrative provides an artificial modulation between the pastoral world, where ballads celebrate an event, and the actualized dream of the tragicomic world, where wonder is enacted onstage. The narrative marks out a step in the transition from an art form which farcically abstracts events from life (Autolycus' ballads, IV.iv.270–82) to the statue scene, which infuses art into life. Autolycus even admits that the wonder of events surpasses his abilities to sell their credibility (V.ii.121–23). The skepticism expressed in this narrative scene exorcises the doubt the audience is likely to feel when the ultimate miracle of Hermione's resurrection is staged.[27] Yet, the comic gentlemen accept the miracles they have seen and their eagerness to witness more miracles readies the audience's sense of wonder. After the gentlemen leave to augment the rejoicing at Paulina's chapel, Autolycus' admission that he could not have made credible Perdita's revelation is another preparation for the immense wonders of the final scene. Autolycus, the confidence man, has been subdued by a greater power than his own for creating "amazement." With this change of a vocal, energetic rogue to a docile and taciturn inferior of the Clown, the play's most skeptical voice is hushed in expectation of miracle.

When Paulina draws the curtain on the statue of Hermione, she notes the decorousness of the change. Whereas the three gentlemen babbled their tale of wonder, the royal party watches the consummate revelation in silence.

> But here it is: prepare
> To see the life as lively mock'd as ever
> Still sleep mock'd death: behold, and say 'tis well.
> [*Paulina draws a curtain, and discovers*
> *Hermione standing like a statue*]
> I like your silence, it the more shows off
> Your wonder: but yet speak; first you, my liege.
> Comes it not something near?
>
> (V.iii.18–23)

Leontes, when pressed to speak, is admiring, but a human touch qualifies his awe: "But yet, Paulina, / Hermione was not so much wrinkled, nothing / So aged as this seems." He

---

[27] C. L. Barber, *Shakespeare's Festive Comedy* (Cleveland, 1963), 232, makes a similar point about Touchstone in *As You Like It*: "The result of including in Touchstone a representative of what in love is unromantic is not, however, to undercut the play's romance: on the contrary, the fool's cynicism, or one-sided realism, forestalls the cynicism with which the audience might greet a play where his sort of realism has been ignored. . . . The net effect of the fool's part is thus to consolidate the hold of the serious themes by exorcising opposition."

looks upon the statue as an *objet d'art* and evaluates it as a thing. The audience, however, is a step ahead of Leontes: the possibility that the statue might actually be Hermione has been suggested in the Third Gentleman's report (V.ii. 93–107). The anachronism of the work's having been "perfected" by a Renaissance artist, Julio Romano, is a signal for the audience to be alert for the revelation, and the Second Gentleman's comments about Paulina's activities in connection with the statue reinforce the clue: "she hath privately twice or thrice a day, ever since the death of Hermione, visited that removed house." Calling attention to the artifice is by this point in the play a familiar sign that appearance and reality may be due for some dislocations. When the curtains reveal Hermione "standing like a statue" we experience the overwhelming surprise of having our still undefined expectations fulfilled. From this point, each perception of Leontes draws him nearer to the recognition that we have already experienced, and the slight distance we gain on his perception allows us the opportunity to evaluate our response by his.[28] In other words, we are caught in that magically double position of being involved in the action and removed from it simultaneously.

The intense beauty of the gradual resurrection of Hermione as she breathes, moves, and finally speaks is heightened by Leontes' intense joy at his growing understanding that the world of settled senses is not the final control of life's events. But the intensity of extreme joy is met with the comic inclusion of Paulina into the play's plane of action. Throughout the play, she has known and controlled the central miracle that informs the entire action. As the stage director, she has remained outside the emotional renewal of the others, carefully controlling the art of the revelation. Now

[28] Cf. Bertrand Evans, *Shakespeare's Comedies* (Oxford, 1960), 314–15.

that her task is successfully completed, she offers to leave the joyful party to their hard-won exultation.

> *Paul.*   Go together,
> You precious winners all; your exultation
> Partake to every one. I, an old turtle,
> Will wing me to some wither'd bough, and there
> My mate (that's never to be found again)
> Lament, till I am lost.
>
> *Leon.*   O, peace, Paulina!
> Thou shouldst a husband take by my consent,
> As I by thine a wife: this is a match
> And made between 's by vows. Thou hast found
> mine;
> But how, is to be question'd; for I saw her,
> As I thought, dead; and have in vain said many
> A prayer upon her grave. I'll not seek far—
> For him, I partly know his mind—to find thee
> An honourable husband. Come, Camillo,
> And take her by the hand; whose worth and
> honesty
> Is richly noted; and here justified
> By us, a pair of kings. Let's from this place.
>
>   (V.iii.130–46)

The final note of reconciliation is appropriately the resumption of Leontes' control over his most unruly subject, Paulina. She procured a wife for him and Leontes procures a husband for her—to replace the one he had sent to his death. Camillo's acquiescence may be as much of a surprise to him as to Paulina, despite Leontes' remark "I partly know his mind." But since Antigonus had earlier been a surrogate victim for Camillo, absorbing the blame and the duty that Leontes would have cast upon Camillo, it is now the best of all comic conclusions to allow Camillo the opportunity to replace Antigonus. Paulina's tongue has a new victim and Leontes is free at last.

This comic reiteration of the stock relationship between

Paulina and Leontes gives a sense of symmetrical completion which the play does not, in fact, supply. The audience does not know any more than Leontes about Hermione's sixteen-year disappearance; but we cannot follow when he says,

> Good Paulina,
> Lead us from hence, where we may leisurely
> Each one demand, and answer to his part
> Perform'd in this wide gap of time, since first
> We were dissever'd: hastily lead away.
>
> (V.iii.151–55)

The omission of an explanation increases our sense of wonder. Logic is frustrated, and, in order to affirm our joyful response to the experience of the play, we are forced to suspend our rational demands for an explanation of cause and effect. Consider, in contrast, the earlier handling of a similar problem in *Much Ado About Nothing*. Hero is slandered, and the Friar suggests that she pretend to be dead (IV.i. 212–45). Like Hermione, Hero returns to life, unexpectedly for Claudio, who believed her dead. But the wonder of Hero's return is reserved for the characters of the play, since the audience is well aware of the logic behind the subterfuge when the Friar plans it. In other words, the earlier play takes great care to explain the practical cause of what would otherwise seem to be miraculous effects, but *The Winter's Tale* does not. Practical explanations are available for its miraculous events, but the dramatic wonder of these events is exploited for the audience to the point that causality no longer seems relevant. *The Winter's Tale* is the only one of Shakespeare's tragicomedies that withholds from the audience the key to the marvelous resolution of the play. This concealment intensifies our immediate experience of dislocation, and it encourages us to alter our perspective in a significant way. We realize, along with the play's characters, that man's actions do not produce irrecoverable effects. The play makes it very clear that a benevolent power has designed and is controlling events to surpass even the hopes and dreams that the man of "settled senses" occasionally entertains. The tragicomic perspective that Shakespeare creates in *The Winter's Tale* forces us to suspend rational judgment so that for a special moment we may glimpse the wonder in the world of human action.

Chapter V ✖✤ THE TEMPEST
"What harmony is this?"

In each of the three plays preceding *The Tempest* the divine controller manifests itself directly. Diana appears to Pericles; Jupiter descends on his eagle in Posthumus' dream-vision; and Apollo is dynamically present in his oracle at Hermione's trial. There is no such direct manifestation in *The Tempest*: Prospero, the magician and the man, incorporates the power and the presence of divinity. The transference of ultimate control to a human actor can be seen also in *The Winter's Tale*, after the reading of the oracle. Paulina asumes the power of director, and she manipulates the play's action toward its final achievement of wonder. If viewed as progressive experiments within a mode, the plays move from the display of supernatural characters to the use of human actors who embody divine powers of control. The merging of two realms becomes a dramatic fact in the character of Prospero rather than in the event of a dream-vision or an oracle. With this change comes a more intense correlation between the controlling figure and the audience. The audience can entertain threats more easily right from the start, because the immediate revelation (I.ii) that Prospero is in control assures us that the threats will be circumvented. In the other three plays that assurance is delayed. For example, the oracle in *The Winter's Tale* promises a happy resolution only after three acts of crisis. The greater security in *The Tempest* allows the audience to concentrate on the fulfillment of the Providential design more than on the crisis of betrayal, which, in fact, happened twelve years before the play begins. *The Tempest* begins at the point of denouement which occurs in the last act of the other three plays. This accounts, in part, for greater unity of action, time, and place than Shakespeare typically observed. Shakespeare seems to have focused on the tragicomic recognition in *The Tempest* almost as if he were defining by greater emphasis the goal toward which his tragicomic methods had been aiming in the earlier plays.[1] The process of dislocation through various kinds of madness, of rebirth after emotional apathy, and of the relocation of an individual's values within a larger scope—all these major emphases of Shakespeare's tragicomic vision are announced and enacted in *The Tempest* with great self-consciousness.

The action of the play primarily concerns the education of the characters to a comprehension of what their tragicomic vision means. The magic island is their schoolroom and Prospero their "schoolmaster" (I.ii.172). The fascination of the play grows in part from Prospero's use of different methods to educate his pupils. Each character or group of characters has special limitations and must be led to the magical vision by a path suited to his individual capacities for perception. The vision itself is defined in the process of coming to it, and the nature of that vision dictates the form of the play. Each motion of *The Tempest*, from the moment of Prospero's reassurance to Miranda that "There's no harm done" (I.ii.14), performs a part of the definition. Like Pericles when he perceives the "rarest dream," like Posthu-

---

[1] See Frank Kermode's comments on the significance of the recognition scene in the last plays, *Shakespeare: The Final Plays* (London, 1963).

mus when he accepts the "speaking such as sense cannot un-tie," and like Leontes when he takes pleasure in the madness that "no settled senses of the world can match," the char-acters in *The Tempest* "rejoice beyond a common joy" (V. i.206–207) only after they have undergone a profound dis-location of their ordinary perspectives.

Prospero defines his methods as he goes, but Shakespeare forces the audience to experience its own dislocation of per-spective before it hears the definition. The first scene, played on a symbolic stage which emphasizes the world's hierarchi-cal structure by its different playing levels, suggests that the storm is not only a natural event, but also a symbol of a dis-located world order. The audience knows both the excite-ment of participating in the immediate physical experience and the anticipation that the storm is an artifice which is directing it toward a larger frame of reference. Miranda's description, which opens the next scene, substantiates the naturalistic interpretation of the storm, but it also creates distance between the experience itself and the perception of it. Prospero's announcement that he has controlled the tem-pest and that no one has been harmed satisfies the anxiety that arises from seeing the storm as a natural event, and, at the same time, it fulfills the expectation that the storm has meaning beyond man's struggle with nature. The audience has thus far experienced three perspectives: its own involve-ment, Miranda's view, and the symbolic view which Pros-pero affirms. Then Ariel appears and describes how he was part of the storm's physical presence:

> I boarded the king's ship; now on the beak,
> Now in the waist, the deck, in every cabin,
> I flam'd amazement: sometime I'd divide,
> And burn in many places; on the topmast,
> The yards and boresprit, would I flame distinctly,
> Then meet and join. Jove's lightnings, the precursors

O' th' dreadful thunder-claps, more momentary
And sight-outrunning were not: the fire and cracks
Of sulphurous roaring the most mighty Neptune
Seem to besiege, and make his bold waves tremble,
Yea, his dread trident shake.

(I.ii.196–206)

With each shift in perspective we feel the security of our
ordinary perceptions slipping away. Having experienced
the dislocation for ourselves, we are then informed of the
method as it is applied to the play's characters. Following
Ariel's descriptive recreation of the storm, Prospero praises
him.

> *Pros.*   My brave spirit!
>   Who was so firm, so constant, that this coil
>   Would not infect his reason?
> *Ari.*   Not a soul
>   But felt a fever of the mad.
>
> (I.i.206–209)

The "fever of the mad" calls all assumptions into question
and is the first step toward recreating man's ability to see.
The prerequisite for rebuilding is destruction, a principle
which the opening shipwreck images. As Gonzalo recognizes in his later speech, adversity brings disorder, out of
which a new order grows: "Was Milan thrust from Milan,
that his issue / Should become Kings of Naples?" (V.i.205–
206). The question is rhetorical, containing its own affirmation of the pattern of reversal leading to renewal. A man
gets used to his way of looking at the world and he adjusts
its diversities to fit his own fixed perspective. But the narrowness of his position is less than he is capable of, even
when, as with Prospero, the fixed position is a learned one.
Prospero's love of books and retirement from his public role
was less than he could achieve in the community of his fellow men. His exile, though it broke the pattern of divinely

sanctioned order, was necessary to reawaken Prospero to the potentials and obligations which only he could fulfill in Milan. The paradox is a familiar one: man must lose his world in order to gain it. The transition from loss to restoration suspends reason and judgment and, throughout the play, is one of the states called madness.

The court group experiences the most complex form of madness that leads to renewal. The positions from which these characters move are established in the opening scene during a moment of physical and psychological stress. The Boatswain ranks between "the mariners" and "the shipmaster" and functions as a median between them as Gonzalo does between Sebastian, Antonio, the two silent courtiers, and the king Alonso. The two median characters also mediate between groups. No chance of communication exists between the arrogant Antonio and Sebastian and the crew, who are concerned only with the practical effort of saving the ship, not with matters of social rank. But Gonzalo, with good humor and patience, attempts to soothe the ruffled feelings of both the Boatswain and the court group. As a man of good sense and right reason, Gonzalo adapts easily to either end of the social scale. He is courtly when he should be, yet jocular in a vulgar vein when the situation demands. We witness his adaptability in such remarks as

Good, yet remember whom thou hast aboard.

I'll warrant him for drowning, though the ship were no stronger than a nutshell, and as leaky as an unstanched wench.

The King and Prince at prayers, let's assist them, For our case is as theirs.

(I.i.19, 46–48, 53–54)

Gonzalo's awareness of decorum in degree is unmistakable, whereas Antonio's and Sebastian's expressions vary predictably in opposition to the ideal role of courtier. In response to the Boatswain's civil request, "I pray now, keep below" (I.i.11), Antonio haughtily reiterates the king's question, "Where is the master?" Such care for apparent rank produces contempt in the Boatswain, who at this point recognizes only the higher order of mastery which controls the elements.[2] From this scene Gonzalo emerges as a calm, although involved, mediator between human factions, sympathetic to all sides, but finally committed to good humor and optimism. In contrast, Antonio and Sebastian are aggressively pessimistic, looking for the worst in every situation, allowing nothing for the value of feelings. Both views condition reality, as we discover in the banter of their next confrontation in Act II.

On dry land (II.i), Gonzalo points out one miracle after another concerning their survival of the storm. Alonso, despairing over the loss of his son, rejects Gonzalo's comfort, and Sebastian and Antonio poke fun at Gonzalo's efforts. Gonzalo is aware of the courtiers' jibes, but he manages to turn them back onto the jesters.

> *Gon.* When every grief is entertain'd that's offer'd,
>   Comes to th' entertainer—
> *Seb.* A dollar.
> *Gon.* Dolour comes to him, indeed: you have spoken truer
>   than you purpos'd.
> *Seb.* You have taken it wiselier than I meant you should.
> *Gon.* Therefore, my lord,—
>
> (II.i.16–22)

2 The Boatswain's tone in "Do you not hear him?" seems clearly sardonic and his sharp reply to Gonzalo's bid for his patience underlines his view: "What cares these roarers for the name of King?" This displacement of political and social order by respect for the manifestation of a higher order's ultimate control directs the audience toward a philosophical question which undergirds the whole play: How truly does the world of human action reflect cosmic order? The fact that Prospero is actually the "master" who controls the tempest makes the Boatswain's questions more dramatically ironic at the same time it complicates the already intricate philosophical question.

The bantering fails to disconcert Gonzalo, but the babble of tongues momentarily drowns the order of his speech and he waits for the merriment to subside. When Adrian remarks on the seeming paradox of the deserted (and therefore barbaric) island's having such a delicate climate, Sebastian and Antonio do what they can to debunk his view and to destroy Gonzalo's premises for deduction when he picks up the argument. Such indiscriminate attack polarizes Antonio and Sebastian as extreme skeptics even more than does the opening scene of the play. Yet their extreme skepticism tends to polarize Gonzalo's optimism as excessive. The verbal sparring about the way the island looks presents two extreme views which demand rational weighing before reality can be estimated.

> *Gon.* Here is everything advantageous to life.
> *Ant.* True; save means to live.
> *Seb.* Of that there's none, or little.
> *Gon.* How lush and lusty the grass looks! how green!
> *Ant.* The ground, indeed, is tawny.
> *Seb.* With an eye of green in 't.
> *Ant.* He misses not much.
> *Seb.* No; he doth but mistake the truth totally.
>
> (II.i.48–55)

Both of Antonio's qualifications of Gonzalo's view merit consideration because our sense of reality demands some deviation from the rule: "everything" is seldom a single quality. The second opposition, like the first, Sebastian mediates: the ground is neither green nor brown, but both, depending upon the conditions the viewer projects onto it. Gonzalo's eye sees a lush and green world because his nature is optimistic and generous; Antonio sees a tawny world because his nature is arid and ingrown.[3]

[3] Antonio is very like Northumberland, whom Edward Hubler describes as the "type" of the "purely villainous" in Shakespeare. See Hubler, "The Economy of the Closed Heart," in Leonard F. Dean (ed.), *Shakespeare: Modern Essays in Criticism* (New York, 1961), 423–24. An-

Despite their attempts to belittle him, Gonzalo persists in viewing their situation hopefully. He points out the miracle of their garments' being as fresh as the day they put them on, in spite of the fact that they have been drenched in the sea: they are "rather new-dyed than stained with salt water." Gonzalo sees the promise of their own miraculous baptism, but Sebastian and Antonio can only laugh at his vision.[4] He apprehends the magic immediately; they require time and trial before they are able to see it. The day they put the garments on was of course the day of "the marriage of the King's fair daughter Claribel to the King of Tunis," a thought which leads them into the banter about the "Widow Dido" and Carthage.

Critics often try to excuse Gonzalo's stupidity in this scene in mistaking Tunis for Carthage. Kermode defends him thus: "At the end of the play we learn Gonzalo's stature; he is not only the good-natured calm old man of the wreck, the cheerful courtier of the second act, and the pure soul of the third; he pronounces the benediction, and we see that he was all the time as right as it was human to be, even when to the common sense of the corrupt he was transparently wrong—wrong about the location of Tunis, wrong about the commonwealth, wrong about the survival of Ferdinand." [5] But it is possible that Gonzalo's identification of Tunis and Carthage should be understood as a conscious

---

tonio treats people as things and only simulates loyalty in order to gain an instrument in Sebastian (II.i.200 ff.). Because he is self-enclosed, Antonio receives neither hurt nor forgiveness from others.

[4] New garments have a powerful theological value in that they may represent a renewed spiritual life. Gonzalo instinctively responds to the potentials of renewal in their return from the sea, while Antonio and Sebastian remain oblivious to their regenerative environment. The play provides other correlatives in terms of the clothing motif which are related either by parody or by parallel.

[5] Frank Kermode, Arden edition, *The Tempest* (London, 1966), xxxviii. See also 46 nn. 78, 84.

metaphor on his part rather than as a literal identification. Throughout the scene he attempts to create for Alonso some sense that their futures are being directed by divine plan. He announces this intention in his first speech to Alonso when he calls their preservation a "miracle." The comparison of Claribel to the "Widow Dido," about which Antonio and Sebastian make such a clamor, may be Gonzalo's conscious effort to provoke Alonso to view their own situation through metaphor. Their course, like that of Aeneas, appears to be harassed by misfortune, but if they are truly like Aeneas, their course is being directed by the gods.[6] Calling Dido a widow causes much jocularity on the part of Antonio and Sebastian, but the audience might recognize in their jests a failure to consider the *Aeneid* itself. Virgil stresses Dido's widowhood throughout the action which concerns her, and Gonzalo's reference to her as a widow suggests that his impression grew from his knowledge of the text itself.[7] But the hilarity which this reference causes

---

[6] Like the *Aeneid*, *The Tempest* begins with a storm at sea and the storm is followed by a long narrative of the history of its main character: Aeneas recounts for Dido the painful battle of Troy and Prospero tells Miranda about the painful conditions of their exile. In addition to the banter about Tunis and Carthage and the "Widow Dido" in II.i, there is the banquet scene, III.iii, which is reminiscent of the *Aeneid*, Book III. Cf. J. M. Nosworthy, "The Narrative Sources of *The Tempest*," *Review of English Studies*, XXIV (1948), 281–94.

[7] When Venus appears disguised as a Tyrian maiden to her son, Aeneas, she tells him of Dido's history and stresses the horror of Sychaeus' murder at the hands of Dido's brother, Pygmalion (Book I). When Dido speaks to Anna, her sister, of her growing interest in Aeneas (Book IV), she recalls her vows to remain faithful to Sychaeus. And when Aeneas deserts her, Dido admits that she deserves to die because she has been faithless to Sychaeus. Finally, when Aeneas approaches her in the lower world (Book VI), Dido turns away and moves "to the shadows / Where Sychaeus, her former husband, took her / With love for love, and sorrow for her sorrow" (Rolfe Humphries' translation, *The Aeneid of Virgil* [New York, 1951], 160). Furthermore, it is likely that Gonzalo would be familiar with the *Aeneid* from having read it, since Prospero implies that Gonzalo's knowledge of books matches his own

in Antonio and Sebastian implies that the popular conception of Dido, then as now, was primarily as the easily won
mistress of Aeneas.[8] If this interpretation is feasible, then
Gonzalo's confusion of Tunis and Carthage does not seem
to be a misinformed error. Adrian pedantically enters the
distinction.

> *Adr.* "Widow Dido" said you? you make me study of
> that: she was of Carthage, not of Tunis.
> *Gon.* This Tunis, sir, was Carthage.
> *Adr.* Carthage?
> *Gon.* I assure you, Carthage.
> *Ant.* His word is more than the miraculous harp.
> *Seb.* He hath rais'd the wall, and houses too.
> *Ant.* What impossible matter will he make easy next?
> *Seb.* I think he will carry this island home in his pocket,
> and give it his son for an apple.[9]

(I.ii.166–68). Gonzalo selected the volumes that Prospero still prizes above
his dukedom.

For other speculations about the meaning of the passage, see John P.
Cutts, "Widow Dido: A Note on *The Tempest*," *American Notes and
Queries*, I (1962–63), 134–35, 150–51; and F. N. Lees, " 'Dido, Queen of
Carthage' and 'The Tempest'," *Notes and Queries*, CCIX (1964), 147–49.
Cutts's suggestion that Sebastian and Antonio may have sung a ballad
called "Queene Dido" which has since dropped from the text seems ex-
cessively interpolative, but I agree with his generalizations concerning
the similarities between the scope of action in the *Aeneid* and in *The
Tempest*.

8 See Arden edition, 47 n. 78.

9 Several expressed puzzlements over this passage have led me to
speculate on it too. I was struck by the close similarity in Dion's aside in
Philaster (IV.ii.149), a play which echoes many brief Shakespearean dia-
logues. Pharamond says, "If I have her not, / By this hand, there shall be
no more Sicily." To which Dion replies in an aside, "What, will he carry
it to Spain in 's pocket?" Another, slightly different parallel occurs in
The White Devil, in the scene of Vittoria Corombona's arraignment.
Monticelso says:

> You see, my lords, what goodly fruit she seems;
> Yet, *like those apples travellers report* [my italics]
> To grow where Sodom and Gomorrah stood,
> I will but touch her, and you straight shall see
> She'll fall to soot and ashes.

J. A. Symonds, *John Webster and Cyril Tourneur: Four Plays* (New

Ant. And, sowing the kernels of it in the sea, bring forth
    more islands.
Gon. Ay.

                         (II.i.78–90)

Adrian's pedantry provokes Gonzalo's insistence on the
identification, and this fact suggests that Gonzalo's tone is
more amused than serious, and that his equation is more a
metaphor than a literal identity. He allows Antonio's and
Sebastian's joke, apparently at his expense, to pass without
argument because his purpose is primarily to distract the
king from his grief, and the courtier's banter has an entertainment value of its own. George Lyman Kittredge, however, considers Gonzalo's "Ay" to be a slow-witted and
foolish affirmation of his earlier remark: "After a pause for
deliberation, Gonzalo thus affirms his statement that Tunis
was Carthage." [10] It is more likely that Gonzalo is simply
humoring the critical courtiers, who insist on making fun of
everything by inverting the speakers' intentions. Knowing
that their kind of wit, which mocks everything, is impossible to combat with protest or reasonable argument, Gonzalo good-naturedly gives in to their play. But Gonzalo's
mildness is not without witty point, and time after time in
this scene he manifests a wit which is nimbler than the broad
humor of Sebastian and Antonio.

York, 1966), 55 (from which I have quoted the passage), cites as a footnote to the "apples" a passage from *Maundeville's Travels*: "And there
besyden growen trees, that beren fulle faire Apples, and faire of colour
to beholde; but whoso brekethe hem, or cuttethe hem in two, he schalle
fynde within hem Coles and Cyndres." G. Wilson Knight cites a possible
parallel from *Antony and Cleopatra* (V.ii.91) in *The Crown of Life*
(London, 1965), 215. All of these parallels suggest that there was a current
joke concerning islands as "pocketable" and the habit of travelers to report their journeys in an exaggerated way. On the latter point, of course,
Antonio provides a footnote (III.iii.26–27).

  [10] George Lyman Kittredge, quoted in Kermode's note, Arden edition,
47–48 n. 90. Kermode apparently agrees with Kittredge since he quotes
without comment.

Another such instance is Gonzalo's famous "commonwealth" speech with its rudely vocal critics in Sebastian and Antonio. The speech follows Alonso's pained outburst that he does not want to think about his daughter's wedding since it was the indirect cause of his son's drowning. Francisco tries to reassure him that Ferdinand may still live, but Sebastian harshly insists that "the fault's your own." Even though Gonzalo agrees that the king is guilty, his humanity forces him to allay the censure; and this brings him to his speech on the commonwealth, which contextually refuses to be taken seriously. Gonzalo's tone is whimsical—that he is aware of possible flaws in his optimistic scheme is apparent—and his motive is pacific. Therefore, in spite of the possibly serious expression of suppressed dreams of anarchy, Gonzalo's situation and attitude preclude a literal interpretation of his speech.[11] When Alonso asks him to cease, "Prithee, no more: thou dost talk nothing to me," Gonzalo quickly agrees.

> *Gon.* I do well believe your highness; and did it to minister occasion to these gentlemen, who are of such sensible and nimble lungs that they always use to laugh at nothing.
> *Ant.* 'Twas you we laughed at.
> *Gon.* Who in this kind of merry fooling am nothing to you: so you may continue, and laugh at nothing still.
> *Ant.* What a blow was there given!
> *Seb.* An it had not fallen flat-long.
> *Gon.* You are gentlemen of brave mettle; you would lift the moon out of her sphere, if she would continue in it five weeks without changing.

> (II.i.167–79)

[11] Critics have often noticed the parallels between Gonzalo's speech on the commonwealth and Montaigne's essay "Of Cannibals." See Kermode's introduction, Arden edition, xxxiv–xxxviii. Margaret T. Hodgen, "Montaigne and Shakespeare Again," *Huntington Library Quarterly*, XVI (1952), 23–41, assembles evidence to suggest sources other than Montaigne.

Antonio is chagrined here, even as Sebastian was earlier (II.i. 21), by Gonzalo's humorous repartee.[12]

The enlarged vision, which Gonzalo demonstrates in embryo with his good-natured observations and imaginative constructs, is pointed more dramatically in the banquet scene, which effectively dislocates the perceptions of the entire court group. The dumb show presentation of the banquet invests the action with symbolic proportions, but no one is certain how to interpret it.

> *Solemn and strange music; and* Prosper *on the top (invisible). Enter several strange Shapes, bringing in a banquet; and dance about it with gentle actions of salutations; and inviting the King, &c., to eat, they depart.*
>
> Alon. What harmony is this? My good friends, hark!
> Gon. Marvellous sweet music!
> Alon. Give us kind keepers, heavens!—What were these?
> Seb. A living drollery. Now I will believe
> That there are unicorns; that in Arabia
> There is one tree, the phoenix' throne; one phoenix
> At this hour reigning there.
> Ant.   I'll believe both;
> And what does else want credit, come to me,
> And I'll be sworn 'tis true: travellers ne'er did lie,
> Though fools at home condemn 'em.
> Gon.   If in Naples
> I should report this now, would they believe me?

12 The wit of Gonzalo's last remark to the two courtiers is almost too subtle. His tone is dryly ironic, using the signal word *brave* to mean "fine or showy" rather than "worthy or courageous," with the implication that underneath an attractive surface corruption festers. The corruption in this case is inconstancy. Lunar control over men's lives was often used as a symbol of Fortune's fickle sway; and Gonzalo's suggestion here seems to be that Sebastian and Antonio would usurp even this control of "chance order," if the regularity of its fluctuating pattern were broken long enough to give them occasion. The enchanted sleep which affects Alonso and company immediately after this remark, indeed, provides Antonio and Sebastian with the opportunity to plot usurpation of the controlling force in the sublunar world.

> If I should say, I saw such islanders,—
> For, certes, these are people of the island,—
> Who, though they are of monstrous shape, yet,
>   note,
> Their manners are more gentle, kind, than of
> Our human generation you shall find
> Many, nay, almost any.
>
> (III.iii.18–34)

For the audience, Prospero's location symbolizes his role as mediator between the mundane world of man's actions and the supermundane world of divine action. But the play's characters cannot see him and must decipher the magic illusion according to their own standards of perception. Antonio and Sebastian are typically extreme in their reactions: if they can believe their eyes, there is no need to discriminate between fact and fancy any longer. Alonso muses upon the ambiguity of the power behind this marvel; and Gonzalo is awed by the gentleness of the spirits' manners. Not until each character has expressed his special sense of awe at the magic scene he has witnessed does Sebastian suggest that Alonso "taste of what is here." Alonso at first refuses, but Gonzalo assures him that there can be no harm in this banquet. The ambiguity of the banquet's meaning tests the nature of each character; and each response defines that nature more fully. Sebastian carelessly suggests that they satisfy their hunger; Alonso mistrusts the possibility of diabolism in the magic (III.iii.20); and Gonzalo, honest and trustworthy himself, suspects nothing evil.[13] When Alonso de-

---

[13] On the critics' problems with this ambiguity, see Northrop Frye's introduction to the Penguin edition of *The Tempest* (Baltimore, 1965), 15 (the banquet is "symbolic of deceitful desires"); Frank Kermode's note on the tradition of the banquet in Christian exegesis, Arden edition, 86 n. 17; and Robert G. Hunter's argument against the weakness of these two interpretations, *Shakespeare and the Comedy of Forgiveness* (New York and London, 1965), 233–34. Hunter suggests that "Prospero's banquet . . . is a type, not of Satan's temptations, but of the commonest of

cides to take a chance and invites the others to "stand to, and do as we," however, Ariel appears in the guise of a Harpy and causes the banquet to vanish. Ariel's primary dramatic purpose is to evoke awe in the courtiers and the king, yet he appears in the role of avenger.[14] He speaks with the voice of an oracle, but he uses the vocabulary of a Christian Providence: "You are three men of sin, whom Destiny,— / That hath to instrument this lower world / And what is in 't,—the never-surfeited sea / Hath caus'd to belch up you" (III.iii.53–56). The conscious "show" of Ariel's artifice emphasizes the fusion of traditions which Prospero's definition of tragicomic action later affirms: "the rarer action is / In virtue than in vengeance" (V.i.27–28). Early Hellenic (and Hebraic) justice—the principle of exact exchange—becomes modified by the Christian doctrine of grace, which in Prospero's human action is the bounty of forgiveness.[15] Ariel's accusation of Alonso follows Alonso's recognition that his perceptions may be inadequate to com-

---

all symbolic banquets: the Communion table." See also Donald K. Anderson, "The Banquet of Love in English Drama (1595–1642)," *Journal of English and Germanic Philology*, LXIII (1964), 422–32. I agree with Hunter that the banquet can hardly be a temptation of the flesh, since Gonzalo approves it and Prospero is its source. As Hunter says, "What occurs when the sinners approach the banquet is not the capitulation of weak men to the blandishments of sensuality, but the prevention of unworthy men from partaking of good things" (234). Mary Ellen Rickey, "Prospero's Living Drolleries," in S. K. Heninger, Jr., Peter G. Philias, and George Walton Williams (eds.), *Renaissance Papers, 1964* (Durham, N.C., 1965), 38–40, also argues that the banquet is presented "to induce consciousness of sin and to provide impetus for repentance."

14 The Harpies in the *Aeneid* descend and smear the banquet with filth because Aeneas has trespassed on their territory and slaughtered their food. The guilt is of a different sort in *The Tempest*. In the larger scheme of action, the Harpies of the *Aeneid* are agents to prevent Aeneas and his men from settling on the wrong soil; they drive them on toward their destined land. Ariel prevents Alonso and the courtiers from securing their limited perception of events and dramatizes the deprivation which they must experience.

15 On the traditional significance of the principle in English drama, see Hunter, *Shakespeare and the Comedy of Forgiveness*.

prehend the fullness of the world about him. Significantly, Gonzalo is excluded from the accusation since he was innocent in the crime of usurpation which has blurred the others' vision of cosmic harmony. He remains to mitigate their despair, but Gonzalo does not undergo the special pain of madness which Alonso experiences: "O, it is monstrous, monstrous!" (III.iii.95). Of the court group, Gonzalo is the only one who does not need to repent before he can see the harmonious vision. But he is unable to understand its fullness until the people with whom his identity is joined realize themselves.

> O, rejoice
> Beyond a common joy! and set it down
> With gold on lasting pillars: in one voyage
> Did Claribel her husband find at Tunis,
> And Ferdinand, her brother, found a wife
> Where he himself was lost, Prospero his dukedom
> In a poor isle, and all of us ourselves
> When no man was his own.
>
> (V.i.206–13)

His summary of the play's action, like most of his observations in earlier scenes, reveals the larger scope of his vision. The order which he recognizes as leading each person to discover his own true nature is macrocosmic: "Look down, you gods, / And on this couple drop a blessed crown! / For it is you that have chalk'd forth the way / Which brought us hither" (V.i.201–204).

While the court party is "knit up / In their distractions" (III.iii.89–90), Prospero turns to his second concern: the union of Ferdinand and Miranda. Their love at first sight is another form of "madness" which dislocates the settled senses of this world. Prospero describes Miranda's state when she falls in love as "infected." The word connects her dislocation of perspective with that which all members of Alonso's party felt during the storm.

> Who was so firm, so constant, that this coil
> Would not infect his reason?
>
> (I.ii.207–208)

> Poor worm, thou art infected!
> This visitation shows it.
>
> (III.i.31–32)

The use of "infect" to mean "affect" is a possibility in this passage,[16] but "visitation" suggests that Miranda's "infected" state is an affliction which Ferdinand is likewise experiencing.[17] Romantic love, even under the most idealized circumstances, receives realistic qualification from Prospero's evaluation. The incipience of love may endanger the operation of rational control, and Prospero cautions Ferdinand about the discord which would result if he allowed passion to sacrifice other values for its own satisfaction (IV.i.15–23). The wedding masque itself includes a reference to the discord inherent in this kind of love. Ceres refuses to join the celebration if Venus and her son are in attendance, but Iris reassures her:

> Of her society
> Be not afraid: I met her deity
> Cutting the clouds towards Paphos, and her son
> Dove-drawn with her. Here thought they to have done
> Some wanton charm upon this man and maid,
> Whose vows are, that no bed-right shall be paid
> Till Hymen's torch be lighted: but in vain.
>
> (IV.i.91–97)

---

[16] C. T. Onions, *A Shakespeare Glossary* (Oxford, 1925), 116, cites examples of this substitution in Shakespeare's other plays.
[17] *Ibid.*, 242. See also Kermode's note, Arden edition, 74.

Prospero's awareness of the dangers which threaten ideal outcomes gives him greater power to shape events according to his design.

Prospero's plan to renew the disordered world of Naples and Milan depends upon the continuation of his lineage through the marriage of Miranda and Ferdinand; and he manipulates the young people in such a way that their attraction is not only immediate but also enduring. In contrast to Alonso's sternness, which, according to Sebastian's biased view (II.i.119–27), forced Claribel to accept the King of Tunis against her wishes, Prospero's sternness in discounting Ferdinand's worth to Miranda only increases her desire to prove him worthy of her love. Prospero's understanding of human resistance to authority gives him an advantage in directing free choice toward the goals he desires. He presents Ferdinand to Miranda in a way that increases their sense of wonder. Ariel prepares Ferdinand for a wondrous revelation by leading him to the scene with mysteriously sweet music. Prospero stages Miranda's first view of Ferdinand in a manner that recalls Paulina's revelation of the statue of Hermione. He instructs Miranda, "The fringed curtains of thine eye advance, / And say what thou seest yond" (I.ii.411–12), and they discuss Ferdinand as if he were an actor on a stage. Miranda's awe is increased through the emphasis on illusory distance, and Ferdinand responds with a conventional assumption that heavenly music accompanies the revelation of a goddess (I.ii.424–30). The hyperbole of the convention, which Shakespeare has used in each of these last plays, is comically pointed by Miranda's modest response that she is "no wonder, sir; / But certainly a maid."

Prospero's pleasure in the working out of his plan for Miranda and Ferdinand seems almost excessive if one considers that love at first sight is the most readily accepted of romantic conventions. Why should Prospero take such care to create a match that needs no outside manipulator? He voices his pleasure in the conventional smoothness of the meeting in several asides during this scene and the next scene in which the lovers meet. His consciousness of Miranda's and Ferdinand's admiration for each other insists on our attention.

> It goes on, I see,
> As my soul prompts it. Spirit, fine spirit! I'll free thee
> Within two days for this.
>
> (I.ii.422–24)

> At the first sight
> They have chang'd eyes. Delicate Ariel,
> I'll set thee free for this.
>
> (I.ii.443–45)

> They are both in either's pow'rs: but this swift business
> I must uneasy make, lest too light winning
> Make the prize light.
>
> (I.ii.453–55)

> [*Aside*] It works. [*To Fer.*] Come on.
> [*To Ariel*] Thou hast done well, fine Ariel!
>
> (I.ii.496–97)

> Poor worm, thou art infected!
> This visitation shows it.
>
> (III.i.31–32)

> Fair encounter
> Of two most rare affections! Heavens rain grace
> On that which breeds between 'em!
>
> (III.i.74–76)

> So glad of this as they I cannot be,
> Who are surpris'd with all; but my rejoicing
> At nothing can be more.
>
> (III.i.92–94)

For Ferdinand and Miranda their love is a complete surprise, but for the audience it is the most familiar kind of magic. Prospero's insistence on theatrics in producing this love match leads us to see it as a contrived illusion rather than as a natural occurrence, however, and this recognition prepares us for the staging of another, less customary magic— the rejuvenation of the human soul. As part of this preparation, Prospero defines an essential component of the sense of wonder which the play evokes: "So glad of this as they I cannot be, / Who are surpris'd with all." [18]

Kermode compares this remark of Prospero's with the line "'Tis new to thee" which qualifies Miranda's "brave new world." [19] Yet Prospero's inability to be as glad as Miranda and Ferdinand at their love depends not on a wiser view of the world which qualifies enthusiasm, but upon the fact that he is not "surprised" by their love as they are. This distinction pinpoints the significance of the other magic actions in the plot. Each character must be caught in amazement, surprised by the reality of a world he has forgotten or never known. Without surprise, the senses remain settled and the important relocation of values does not occur. This play in particular Shakespeare has built upon the tutorial method of presenting an action first and then defining its meaning. The tragicomic experience he attempts to provide in all of the last plays depends upon the simultaneous awareness of involved participation and rational, "distanced" perception of what that participation means.

The suspension of resolution which delays judgment is another facet of this experience, causing the characters in the play and the audience watching the play to live out the

[18] I have followed the Folio reading of this line, rather than Lewis Theobald's generally accepted conjecture, "withal." See Arden edition, 77 n. 93.
[19] Arden edition, 124 n. 184.

experience of Patience, which outside the play remains an abstraction rather than an action. The realization of concepts in experience is the crucial, didactic point of the final plays, and Patience is a central concept that takes on flesh. Prospero leaves Alonso and the courtiers in suspended states not only because he has other dramatic matters to attend to, but also because in this suspension of reason and action they are being prepared for rebirth.

> My high charms work,
> And these mine enemies are all knit up
> In their distractions: they now are in my power;
> And in these fits I leave them.
> (III.iii.88–91)
> A solemn air, and the best comforter
> To an unsettled fancy, cure thy brains,
> Now useless, boil'd within thy skull! There stand,
> For you are spell-stopp'd. . . .
> . . . The charm dissolves apace;
> And as the morning steals upon the night,
> Melting the darkness, so their rising senses
> Begin to chase the ignorant fumes that mantle
> Their clearer reason. . . .
> . . . Their understanding
> Begins to swell; and the approaching tide
> Will shortly fill the reasonable shore,
> That now lies foul and muddy.[20]
> (V.i.58–82)

---

[20] Compare the imagery of ebb and flow in this passage with Antonio's and Sebastian's use as they plot to murder Alonso and Gonzalo (II.i.214–26). Because images which concern the moon and the sea are so insistent in relation to the various types of madness (lunacy), the use of the ebbing tide to describe the fallen spiritual state of Sebastian and Antonio (and later, Alonso) carries a complex symbolic impact. A later Catholic application of the image may be found in the emblem of "The Moone" in *Partheneia Sacra* (1633), quoted in Rosemary Freeman, *English Emblem Books* (London, 1948), 198:

THE POESIE.

The Empresse of the Sea, *Latona* bright,
Drawes like a load-stone by attractiue might
The Oceans streames, which having forward runne

Miranda passes through a similar period of enforced suspension of perception before she is allowed to meet Ferdinand. Prospero makes clear the fact that his magic powers have caused Miranda's drowsiness and that he has planned her sleep to prepare her for the miraculous experience of falling in love (I.ii.184–86, 307–308). Before he allows her to see Ferdinand, however, Prospero leads her to look at Caliban. Their encounter prepares Miranda further to see the goodness of Ferdinand by contrast to the meanness of that "abhorred slave"; Prospero leaves nothing to chance in preparing his pupils to make what seems to be their free choice. The spell of Alonso and the court group differs from Miranda's, but the experiences of both are similar enough to suggest that Prospero's actions adhere to a conscious design. With or without guilt, the characters undergo a suspension of perception in which their ability to see is renewed. Miranda's sleep and awakening is a simplified and innocent version of the "madness" and rebirth which the king and his group endure.[21]

> Calls back againe, to end where they begunne.
> The Prince of darknes had ecclipsed *Eues* light,
> And Mortals, clowded in Cymmerian night,
> Were backwards drawne by *Eue*, as is the Maine;
> 'Twas only *Marie* drew to God agine:
> O chast Diana, with thy siluer beames,
> Flux & reflux (as in the Oceans streames)
> 'Tis thou canst cause. O draw! and draw me so,
> That I in vice may ebbe, in Vertue flow.

[21] Throughout the play sleep is an important and multivalent motif. Like Miranda's drowsiness, the heaviness which induces Alonso and the court group to sleep (II.i.183 ff.) is caused by magic which does not affect Antonio and Sebastian. They remain awake and plot the king's death. Caliban also plots to kill Prospero while he sleeps (III.ii.85 ff.), in parody of Antonio's and Sebastian's thwarted plan. Caliban's famous description of the "sweet airs" of the island (III.ii.133–41) mingles the experiences of waking and dreaming and displays surprising sensitivity. His confusion of the two states resembles Prospero's intentional mingling of them in his analogy: "We are such stuff / As dreams are made on; and our little life / Is rounded with a sleep" (IV.i.156–58). The Boatswain's description of the mariners' dreaming sleep shows the same confusion of perspective

The experience of madness and rebirth is a shattering one, and Alonso at first hesitates to accept the new world as real. When Prospero presents himself dressed in ducal clothing, Alonso requires reassurance that he is not mad, knowing, as did Leontes, that the world of settled senses does not contain such miracles (V.i.111–19). Prospero delays an explanation, however, and increases his audience's sense of wonder as he reveals Ferdinand and Miranda "playing at chess." Their tableau momentarily stops the action, and the static picture suggests a symbolic concord of reason and passion in romantic love.[22] The values expressed in their brief speeches which follow their discovery, however, are strangely contradictory to the idealized vision.[23] Miranda expresses a rather worldly cognition of Ferdinand's hidden motives, which seems to contradict her almost absolute lack of experience in the world where such social subtleties are learned.

> *Mir.* Sweet lord, you play me false.
> *Fer.*   No, my dearest love,
>   I would not for the world.
> *Mir.* Yes, for a score of kingdoms you should wrangle,
>   And I would call it fair play.
>
>   (V.i.172–75)

that the others have experienced (V.i.229–40). At different times, sleep seems to be a return to innocence (in that one is vulnerable and unaware of threats); a healing process that "knits up the ravell'd sleave of care"; a period of confused perceptions; and a preface to the experience of miracle.

[22] Chess requires the exercise of reason and it was traditionally associated with medieval courtship. See H. J. R. Murray, *A History of Chess* (Oxford, 1913), 436–37. Rickey, "Prospero's Living Drolleries," 36–37, cites several significant uses of the symbolic chess game within the medieval and Renaissance Christian tradition.

[23] Chaucer's black knight in *The Book of the Duchess* describes how he lost a game of chess to Lady Fortune, who slyly "tok my fers"; but he realizes that guile is to be expected in playing the game: see F. N. Robinson's edition, *The Works of Geoffrey Chaucer* (Cambridge, Mass., 1957), 273, lines 673–78.

There is almost a reversal in the positions of the two lovers from the earlier scene (III.i.37–59) in which Ferdinand speaks at some length of his experience with "several women" in order to insist that Miranda is "peerless," and in which Miranda protests her ignorance of womankind. Her recognitions in the lines that accompany the chess game possess the subtlety of understanding that usually grows from experience rather than from instinct, and Ferdinand's protestation of fidelity is absolute in ignoring possible qualifications by the world which he has already known. Yet this is only one part of the vision which is caught in the complex balance of contradiction.

When Alonso voices a fear that the scene may prove to be another "vision of the island," he points to a paradox. Ferdinand and Miranda are real and their appearance is not, like the vanishing banquet, a magical illusion. But they are, in another sense, the true "vision" which the magic island has created because they image the harmony of merging worlds. Ferdinand and Miranda represent not only a fusion of the world of Naples and the world of the island, but with the masque of celebration in the immediate dramatic past, their betrothal brings into the same plane of action the world of gods and the world of man. Prospero's art effects the fusion, but the final vision transcends his art. In each display of his magic or of his art prior to the final vision, the action has been left suspended or has been cut short. The dramatic utility of this practice is, of course, to increase the wonder of the final vision, but symbolically it suggests that art alone cannot induce true harmony. Men also must choose to actualize their own latent goodness before they can comprehend the larger benevolence of the world in which they move. In other words, the concept of universal harmony can be known only through the experience of achieving harmony in human actions. The pattern of order perennially exists, but it realizes the ideal possibility only in its enactment. The "vision of the island" remains anchored in the actual by means of ironic qualifications which acknowledge man's inability to sustain perfection even as it is achieved. Such is the effect of Prospero's response to Miranda's wonder at

> How many goodly creatures are there here!
> How beauteous mankind is! O brave new world,
> That has such people in 't!
>
> (V.i.182–84)

The laconic quality of Prospero's "'Tis new to thee" balances the expansiveness of Miranda's praise. And though this world's "newness" is the aspect which Prospero's remark qualifies, the obvious irony of describing Sebastian and Antonio as "beauteous mankind" is a powerful qualification of Miranda's point of view as well. Despite Prospero's forgiveness of the pair, Sebastian and Antonio have not been repaired in dramatic action sufficiently to override their earlier characterizations.[24] A further balance of Miranda's enthusiasm is the parody which Caliban provides when, like a coda to the vision, Ariel drives him in with Stephano and Trinculo. His immediate reaction to his first sight of the assembled court party is very like Miranda's in spite of his own particular frame of reference: "O Setebos, these be brave spirits indeed! / How fine my master is!" (V.i.261–62). Both of their responses to the "brave" newness of the court world recall an earlier parallel between Miranda's response to Ferdinand (I.ii.412–14, 420–21), and Caliban's response to Stephano and Trinculo (II.ii.117–19). In the final

---

[24] The manner in which Prospero forgives them has something to do with this (V.i.74–79, 126–34). Antonio's silence and Sebastian's near-silence, except for his "A most high miracle" (V.i.177) and some final banter at the expense of Stephano and Trinculo, do not effect the restoration of their characters. In contrast, Alonso's expressions of pain, guilt, and joy do restore him.

scene, however, when Caliban recognizes his former stupidity in celebrating such fools as "brave gods," his comprehension, which was so long in coming, qualifies the entire
pattern of his and Miranda's enthusiasms for the "brave new
world" and its creatures.[25]

Throughout the play Caliban and his pair of "gods" provide a balance for the awe and completeness of the more
serious actions. There are few themes or images or attitudes
which the drunken trio do not present again on a parodic
level. Trinculo and Stephano are as astonished by Caliban's
appearance as he is by theirs. The wonder which they express over each other parallels Ferdinand's admiration for
Miranda and her astonishment at seeing such a "brave" and
"noble" form. Worldliness and ignorance meet on the common level of wonder in both cases, but the ethereal and "romantic" quality that Ferdinand and Miranda expand upon
is alloyed with the baseness of Caliban's encounter with
Trinculo and Stephano.

Both Antonio and Caliban recruit someone to carry out
their villainy,[26] and both are defeated by the comic inade-
quacies of their accomplices as well as by Prospero's controlling magic. While the king and Gonzalo sleep, Antonio
persuades Sebastian that conscience is a thing that can be
put aside, and Sebastian agrees to follow Antonio's example.

---

[25] Newness itself is a contradictory concept here, implying simultaneously rebirth and ignorance. The different levels of meaning attached
to the word *brave* throughout the play also permit Miranda's evaluation
more irony than she is aware of. See, too, Stephen K. Orgel, "New Uses
of Adversity: Tragic Experience in *The Tempest*," in Reuben A. Brower
and Richard Poirier (eds.), *In Defense of Reading* (New York, 1962),
121–22, 132, for comments on the pairing of Caliban and Miranda and on
Prospero's qualification of Miranda's vision.

[26] Antonio's guilt and present treachery, like Caliban's parody, act as
buffers to Alonso's guilt in the usurpation of Prospero. The king is protected from final censure because of the presence of Antonio and Caliban
in much the same way that Leontes receives protection from Paulina and
Antigonus, and Posthumus from Cloten.

Seb.   Thy case, dear friend,
      Shall be my precedent; as thou got'st Milan,
      I'll come by Naples. Draw thy sword: one stroke
      Shall free thee from the tribute which thou payest;
      And I the King shall love thee.
Ant.   Draw together;
      And when I rear my hand, do you the like,
      To fall it on Gonzalo.
Seb.   O, but one word. [*They talk apart.*]
                               (II.i.285–91)

Sebastian's hesitation following his firm decision comically deflates the moment for action before Ariel even appears "[*invisible*]" to awaken Gonzalo to the danger. The device of calling characters aside so that some other stage business can be accomplished without their knowledge is a common artifice in the last plays. Its obviousness as a device is farcical, particularly in situations which are generating serious threats. In *Cymbeline*, for example, when the Queen is plotting to poison Imogen, she calls Pisanio aside—"Hark thee, a word" (I.vi.32)—and the doctor delivers a soliloquy to reveal that the drug he has given her is not poison. This reassures the audience that the Queen's evil will not be accomplished, and the comedy thus contains her threat. Another example occurs in *The Winter's Tale* after Polixenes has delivered his ultimatum to Florizel and Perdita. Florizel draws Perdita aside—"Hark, Perdita"—and says to Camillo, "I'll hear you by and by" (IV.iv.507–508). Camillo then suggests his plan for achieving a harmonious resolution. There is no dramatic need for Camillo's brief soliloquy, but its self-conscious stress on artifice distances the situation and reduces the threat of Florizel's exile to comedy.[27] Sebastian's aside

---

[27] The device is repeated a few lines later when Camillo calls Florizel aside to leave the stage open for Autolycus' soliloquy, IV.iv.595. For a discussion of the device in this sequence, see Nevill Coghill, "Six Points of Stage-Craft in *The Winter's Tale*," *Shakespeare Survey*, XI (1958), 31–41.

accomplishes the same effect. The murder of the king is serious business for a tragicomedy, and keeping the tone keyed to a middle pitch requires skill. Through the use of patent artifice Shakespeare is able to release anxiety from the situation at the same time he points up the moral decay of the Neapolitan world. Sebastian and Antonio reenact the pre-play crisis of Prospero's betrayal and exile when they plot to kill Alonso. Because Prospero is in control of their actions on the island, their plot slips into a comic analogue of the earlier usurpation. In turn, Caliban's plot against Prospero is a parody which exorcises the entire pattern of usurpation through farcical action. This gradual reduction of evil threat to farcical inertia (IV.i.194–254) allows the inclusion of Antonio, Sebastian, and Caliban in the harmonious vision.

Whereas neither set of conspirators is able to seize the opportune moment to accomplish their plans, Prospero, working within the Providential design, grasps the moment for action. As he explains to Miranda in their opening dialogue, he too depends on powers other than his own.

> . . . by my prescience
> I find my zenith doth depend upon
> A most auspicious star, whose influence
> If now I court not, but omit, my fortunes
> Will ever after droop.
>
> (I.ii.180–84)

His very dependence increases the strength of his choice. As former Duke of Milan he passively allowed his usurpation, but as king of the island and the source for his subjects' restoration, he maintains his purpose actively. Prospero makes other statements, usually in connection with Caliban, that reveal his less than absolute power, and these statements increase dramatic tension for an otherwise predetermined action. All along Caliban has been Prospero's one reminder of his own limitations. Prospero recounts how, on first coming to the island, he took Caliban under his care and tried to teach him the ways of reason:

> I have us'd thee,
> Filth as thou art, with human care; and lodg'd thee
> In mine own cell, till thou didst seek to violate
> The honour of my child.
>
> (I.ii.347–50)

Caliban's nature remained unregenerate and Prospero no longer hopes that his magic or his art can teach him anything except the fear of punishment. That Prospero feels the threat of Caliban's unregenerate nature to be real is obvious in his aside that explains his interruption of the wedding masque:

> I had forgot that foul conspiracy
> Of the beast Caliban and his confederates
> Against my life: the minute of their plot
> Is almost come.
>
> (IV.i.139–42)

Miranda and Ferdinand comment on his agitation and reveal through their remarks the uniqueness of his "distemper." In order to calm their anxiety, Prospero explains the vanishing vision with his famous speech which draws an analogy between art and life. He concludes, however, with an important admission.

> Sir, I am vex'd;
> Bear with my weakness; my old brain is troubled:
> Be not disturb'd with my infirmity:
> If you be pleas'd, retire into my cell,
> And there repose: a turn or two I'll walk,
> To still my beating mind.
>
> (IV.i.158–63)

A troubled brain and a beating mind are signs of transformation in the other characters of the play, and the fact that

Prospero can still be so troubled signifies that he too may be undergoing a kind of metamorphosis. The report from Ariel which describes his leading of Caliban, Trinculo, and Stephano into the "filthy-mantled pool" arouses again Prospero's angry assumption that Caliban cannot be saved.

> A devil, a born devil, on whose nature
> Nurture can never stick; on whom my pains,
> Humanely taken, all, all lost, quite lost;
> And as with age his body uglier grows,
> So his mind cankers.
>
> (IV.i.188–92)

Prospero's personal investment in Caliban's "nurture" is the source of his present anger and sorrow. He has failed both by persuasion and by force to change Caliban's view of the world or his pleasure in corruption. It is a humbling recognition for Prospero, and one which qualifies the power of his art to harmonize the world. Even so, Prospero gives up too soon. Immediately following his admission of absolute failure and permanent disappointment, Caliban shows a power of reason at least superior to that of the corrupt "civilized" response of Stephano and Trinculo when he sees through the trick of the glittering clothes. Although Caliban directs his wit in this case to the destruction of Prospero, the fact that he has any is mitigating. In the final scene, when Caliban sees the difference between his false gods and his true master, he too understands the values of a renewed and re-ordered world.

> I'll be wise hereafter,
> And seek for grace. What a thrice-double ass
> Was I, to take this drunkard for a god,
> And worship this dull fool!
>
> (V.i.294–97)

Caliban's limitations as a pupil have been so severe that Prospero despaired of his capacity to learn. But Caliban does finally see the difference between Stephano and Prospero and he sees it so firmly that his vision contradicts Prospero's preceding remark that Caliban cannot learn anything. Prospero's foreknowledge has been incomplete. His prescience did not include Caliban's learning; but Caliban learns, as the others do, by experience rather than by precept.[28] As a result, Prospero himself experiences some "surprise." The resolution which includes more than even he had foreseen rebinds him, like Paulina of *The Winter's Tale*, into the plane of action on which the other characters exist. His entire relationship with Caliban humanizes Prospero by revealing his limitations as a mage as well as his difficulty in acknowledging "this thing of darkness" as his own (V.i.275).

Their relationship of mutual frustration is a foil for Prospero's relationship with Ariel, and it functions as a parodic balance. In contrast to Caliban's dramatic utility as a threat to Prospero's safety, Ariel is a dramatic tool which fulfills Prospero's plans. Ariel creates the tempest, leads all the characters about the island, performs various roles in the banquet and in the masque, and sings and plays "sweet airs" of the island. He is everywhere, performing whatever Prospero demands as quickly as the wink of an eye or the beat of a pulse. Ariel is the "actor" absolute: having no determined personality of his own, he is capable of playing any role. Prospero, as stage director, appreciates fully the value of having such a versatile actor to cast. Their relationship self-consciously points to the analogy of the actor-director bond

[28] Caliban, like the others who learn through experience, also suffers an unsettling of the senses. Ariel describes leading the trio to the "filthy-mantled pool" in terms of synesthesia:

> Then I beat my tabor;
> At which, like unback'd colts, they prick'd their ears,
> Advanc'd their eyelids, lifted up their noses
> As they smelt music.
>   (IV.i.175–78)

in the theater. Whenever Ariel finishes a performance, he proudly asks for Prospero's approval; and Prospero soothes Ariel's actor's vanity with enthusiastic praise.[29] When Prospero rejoins the other characters in their fiction, his final gesture as stage director is to release his artist: "My Ariel, chick, / That is thy charge: then to the elements / Be free, and fare thou well!" (V.i.316–18). Even Prospero's reprimands, when Ariel grows weary of performing, resemble the kind of psychological manipulation that a director might use on a temperamental actor.

> *Ari.* Is there more toil? Since thou dost give me pains,
> Let me remember thee what thou hast promis'd,
> Which is not yet perform'd me.
> *Pros.*   How now? moody?
> What is't thou canst demand?
> *Ari.*   My liberty.
> *Pros.* Before the time be out? no more!
>
> (I.ii.241–46)

The play has a given performance time, and the chief actor cannot quit before it is done.

Both Ariel and Caliban want to gain their freedom, but only Ariel is willing to earn his. Caliban's song after he has substituted Stephano for Prospero brings into focus the whole question of freedom and liberation in the play.

> *'Ban, 'Ban, Cacaliban*
> *Has a new master:—get a new man.*
> Freedom, high-day! high-day, freedom! freedom,
> high-day, freedom!
>
> (II.ii.184–87)

Absolute freedom only Ariel can take; it is a paradoxical concept for the rest of the characters, just as Caliban's drunken song inadvertently defines it. True freedom de-

[29] See, for example, I.ii.193–206, 318–20, 497–98; III.iii.83–86; IV.i.35–37; V.i.240–41.

pends upon the proper relationship between privilege and obligation. The master must exert control over his servant in order that the servant fulfill his role properly, and the servant must bend to his superior's will. But the maintenance of such control is not easy, as Prospero's outbursts at both Caliban and Ariel indicate (I.ii.257 ff., 347 ff.). In order to achieve freedom both the master and the servant must give up personal privilege to some extent. Caliban does not perceive his obligation in the bond between master and servant although he does perceive his dependent position; he wants all the privilege and no work. Therefore, he thinks by adopting a master who is less stern he can enjoy more freedom. He is accurate in saying that a "new master" makes a "new man" because the mutual bond transmits such shaping influence. But he is mistaken in hoping that the lack of responsibility breeds freedom. For both Caliban and Ariel the process of achieving freedom is more significant than the actuality. Caliban attempts to grasp freedom in an inverted way and by negation he defines it; Ariel, after one threatening reminder from Prospero of his former confinement, demonstrates the proper definition and ultimately achieves it.

Ariel's reward is not without its pain, at least for Prospero. Caliban pains him because he will not learn, but Ariel learns so well that he wins the right to separate from his master. Throughout the play, despite his various spirit guises, Ariel approaches a human nature. When he reports on the confinement of the court group and notes Gonzalo's tears, he tells Prospero:

> Your charm so strongly works 'em,
> That if you now beheld them, your affections
> Would become tender.
> *Pros.*   Dost thou think so, spirit?
> *Ari.*   Mine would, sir, were I human.
>
> (V.i.17–20)

And when he sings as he helps Prospero into his ducal clothing a little later, Prospero is so touched that he says, "Why,
that's my dainty Ariel! I shall miss thee; / But yet thou shalt
have freedom" (V.i.95–96). Prospero's final lines suggest
the same mixture of happiness and nostalgia (V.i.316–18).
Prospero's fondness for Ariel actually humanizes Prospero
more than it does Ariel, because Ariel's energies are primarily directed toward his final liberation. Nonetheless, there is
an almost human relationship between them which makes
the freeing of Ariel a qualified joy. It seems that Prospero
does not simply equate Ariel with his magic power, but that
he also views him as an independent being, capable of learning and of understanding.[30] Ariel is metaphysically transformed from sprite into element in a manner that images the
other transformations in the play. The characters who learn
who they are and what their relationships mean are changed
by a less drastic metamorphosis which liberates them as well.
But the cost of transformation qualifies the joy for Prospero.

While he has provided for the transformation of the
others, Prospero himself has undergone a kind of metamorphosis. His first appearance prepares for his final renuncia-
tion of his magic powers. Having reassured Miranda that
his tempest has done no harm, Prospero removes his magic
robes—"Lie there, my Art"—while he narrates the history
of their expulsion from Milan (I.ii.23–25). Putting aside
his magic garment signifies Prospero's transformation from
mage to man, and his following narrative emphasizes two
significant human limitations. One is his own dependence
upon seizing the moment for action (I.ii.180–84), and the
other is his repeated nudging of Miranda's attention. The

---

[30] In a similar way the separation of the audience from the tragicomic
vision presented on the stage brings with it a sense of loss. We have in-
vested imaginative energy in Prospero and his play, and we are now re-
quired to release him, as he releases Ariel "to the elements."

first point, aside from insisting on Prospero's humanity, establishes him as the chosen mediator between a higher order and the realm of man's actions. As an exemplar of redeemed action, Prospero must represent mankind in its human limitations; a god acting as man has too great an advantage for dramatic effectiveness in escaping the ultimate restrictions which man's frailty places upon his actions. If Prospero fails to seize this unique moment in which to act, the whole of his plan to redeem his past will fail and his "fortunes will ever after droop." As if to reiterate his human limitations, Prospero narrates his history in the manner of a vain schoolmaster who is comically jealous of Miranda's attention. He persistently calls her attention to his narrative when it is obviously not necessary.

I pray thee, mark me.	67
Dost thou attend me?	78
Thou attend'st not?	87
I pray thee, mark me.	88
Dost thou hear?	106

Miranda's response to all these demands for attention is that her attention is riveted upon him: "Your tale, sir, would cure deafness." There are, of course, other dramatic purposes in having Prospero make these excessive demands,[31] but one of the effects is to humanize his characterization by insisting on his vanity. He is proud of his pupil whom he has nurtured and when she asks the proper leading question—"Wherefore did they not / That hour destroy us?"—Prospero shows his pride, both in the aptness of her question

[31] One important purpose is to break up the monotony of a long narrative for both of Prospero's audiences. Kermode points out, Arden edition, lxxv, that this scene conforms to the *protasis* in an "academic theory of structure"; and Bernard Knox, "*The Tempest* and the Ancient Comic Tradition," in W. K. Wimsatt, Jr. (ed.), *English Stage Comedy*, English Institute Essays, 1954 (New York, 1955), 61, calls the scene "a typical Plautine delayed prologue." Perhaps Prospero is even a bit nervous about exposing his past actions to Miranda's judgment.

and in the narrative skill which has led her to ask it: "Well demanded, wench: / My tale provokes that question" (I.ii. 139–40). Withholding such information creates suspense, not only for Miranda but for the audience who is watching this tutorial. In a larger use of the same method, he leads Miranda to ask his reasons for creating the tempest, but he avoids a full explanation (I.ii.177–84). He assures her (and the audience) that it was performed toward a good end, but he leaves the unfolding of its true purpose to the action of the play. Prospero's vanity as a teacher is justified: he is able to lead all of his pupils to experience that vision which he foreknows, at the same time he allows them to choose their own direction.

Another indication that Prospero himself undergoes a change of attitude is the arresting present tense of his narrative when he tells how Gonzalo "furnish'd me / From mine own library with volumes that / I prize above my dukedom" (I.ii.166–68). Although he has determined on "virtue" rather than "vengeance," Prospero enjoys his intellectual power in a very human way. One of the original causes of his usurpation, his interest in books above an active public life, has still to undergo modification. The movement from "volumes that I prize" to "I'll drown my book" is Prospero's penance through action. He does not withdraw from the propitious moment. His activity in bringing his enemies to repentance depends upon his theurgic power and for most of his actions he wears the magic robe. But in the final scene he changes this garment for his ducal clothing, and the last "vision" which he presents—the vision of all the characters reconciled—does not depend upon his magic charms.

Prospero thus changes from magician to man before our eyes as he puts off and takes on the clothing appropriate to each role. His vanity, his affections, even his irascibility reintegrate him into the human level of action. But his final gesture, the Epilogue, seals the transition.

> Now my charms are all o'erthrown,
> And what strength I have's mine own,
> Which is most faint: now, 'tis true,
> I must be here confin'd by you,
> Or sent to Naples.
>
> (Epil., 1–5)

Prospero gives his audience the ultimate control. Their imagination becomes the magician; they are now the master of the mage, and his ability to realize his proper role as Duke of Milan depends upon their "indulgence."

The Epilogue exists on so many levels simultaneously that its power is bound to exceed any attempts to define it. On its simplest level, it is a clever bid for applause and the compliment Prospero pays his audience is a conventional courtesy. Yet this literal plea for applause becomes a profound metaphor for the entire action of the play. Prospero's first few lines summarize the transition from a magic island to an actual world in which the audience itself lives. The magic has ceased to be an illusion; it has become an actual power which the audience knows as its own—the power of imagination. That imagination has been actively engaged for the few hours of the play's performance so that the process of confining it to the everyday world is a difficult adjustment, possibly somewhat painful. A beautiful vision, no matter how illusory, is not easy to give up. Prospero is providing a means, indeed a necessity, for keeping that vision alive.

> Let me not,
> Since I have my dukedom got,
> And pardon'd the deceiver, dwell
> In this bare island by your spell.

The island is now "bare" because it has been depleted of its imaginative "plantation" (II.i.139). Its people have seen its vision and are carrying it back to Naples. So Prospero is asking his audience to do. The liberation for each man to be himself, sure of his meaning in the Providential order, depends upon the audience's acceptance of that order. If they sever the play from their own experience, allowing "suspension of disbelief" only for the duration of the play, they are confining Prospero to his island—his magic did not work. In effect, they are saying that his fiction is very well and good for a play, but it is only a fiction. On the other hand, if they recognize the perdurable truths of the fiction as metaphor for their own actuality, and carry the vision of the play into their own lives, they will release Prospero to go to Naples and realize his own proper identity as Duke of Milan. This kind of didacticism, which demands that the audience accept the poetic lie as truth, is common to all the final plays, but it comes closest to full articulation in *The Tempest*. The imagination can look through the sphere of art into a metaphysical realm that fuses all experience—the ideal as well as the actual—into a pattern of reality. The tragicomic vision of all these plays affirms and revitalizes the imaginative life, and the experience brings the playwright and his audience into a spiritual community which remains active long after the playhouse darkens.

Chapter VI ✣ THE WORLD
OF WONDER

The problem of educating our responses so that they are adequate for the drama Shakespeare has given us is a perennial one, but it is especially acute in respect to the late plays. We cannot fully appreciate the way in which Shakespeare shaped his materials in these plays until we realize that he was moving experimentally into relatively unexplored dramatic territory. A genre as indeterminate as tragicomedy must have presented a tremendous challenge to the playwright in many areas, and teaching the audience a new set of expectations must have been one of the major problems. Modern audiences have often failed to see that Shakespeare's tragicomic goals differ from his aims in other modes, and, because of this, they tend to misjudge his achievements in these last plays.

Guarini's definition of tragicomedy might well be read as an appraisal of Shakespeare's work in the genre: "For he who makes tragicomedy does not intend to compose separately either a tragedy or a comedy, but from the two a third thing that will be perfect of its kind." [1] The "third thing" in Shakespeare's plays results from the balancing of

[1] Giambattista Guarini, quoted in Allan H. Gilbert, *Literary Criticism: Plato to Dryden* (New York, 1940), 507.

motions toward the ideal and the actual, toward the artificial and the natural, toward sadness and joy. These contradictory impulses which the audience experiences simultaneously dislocate typical perspectives and force judgment to wait for the play's concluding vision. The tension of suspended judgment relaxes into joyful resolution only after we have experienced multiple points of view.

Many critics have tended to discount the importance of ambivalent perspectives in these plays. In general, they celebrate the "mystic" vision which transcends concerns of everyday existence, and they devalue the obviousness of the theatrical devices Shakespeare uses. The crucial point they have missed is that these responses, apart from the praise and blame attached to them, are simultaneously valid: the mysterious exists in the obvious (Jupiter descends on a mechanical eagle), and the sublime achieves meaning under the terms provided by the ridiculous. For example, Caliban's ignorance clarifies Miranda's innocence, and her ideal purity takes a living place in the reordered society because it has been defined and qualified by his degenerate nature.

Criticism which fails to distinguish between Shakespeare's goals in the tragicomedies and those of his other plays falsifies his achievement. Even in generic criticism, a preference for tragedy, for comedy, or for chronicle plays may encourage the judgment that the late plays reveal a falling off in Shakespeare's artistic control. Although Guarini's opinion that tragicomedy is the highest form of dramatic composition may be overenthusiastic,[2] it represents a salutary balance for critical attitudes that dismiss tragicomedy as a frivolous and unimportant genre.

The pattern of dramatic action which repeatedly evokes

---

[2] *Ibid.*, 512: "truly if today men understood well how to compose tragicomedy (for it is not an easy thing to do), no other drama should be put on the stage."

wonder in the play's characters and audience makes it clear that for Shakespeare tragicomedy had significance. His attempts to create his tragicomic vision vary with each play, almost as if he were purposefully exploring different paths toward the same goal. In *Pericles*, there is great stress on antique devices, such as Gower, the dumb shows, and the tournaments. *Cymbeline* juggles the traditions of romance, pastoral, and history in such a way that the play's action points up the limitations of all formulaic approaches to life's complexities. The stock characterizations in *The Winter's Tale*, especially in the relationship of Paulina and Leontes, exert contradictory pressures against narrative situations. *The Tempest* is in many ways Shakespeare's dramatic definition of tragicomedy, and Prospero acts as a Providential surrogate, very much like a stage director or a playwright, who leads the characters and the audience toward tragicomic vision.

The change from direct supernatural manifestation of divine control to a human embodiment of it is only one of many progressive patterns in these plays. This development correlates with another: the change from the almost totally passive hero in Pericles to the thoroughly active hero, Prospero, who is responsible for consequences because he participates in Providential knowledge. While the protagonists' actions differ in motive and in meaning, the point stressed is the same: human causes do not create irreversible effects in the world of Shakespeare's tragicomedy. Only when the human actor realizes his participation in the realm of divine power are the consequences of his actions meaningful.

Other patterns of characterization suggest that Shakespeare was experimenting with different ways of handling the stereotyped figures that are a basic material of tragicomedy. In *Pericles* and *Cymbeline*, for example, there is a jealous and evil queen who encourages evil in others. Cleon and Cymbeline are sketchily realized in comparison to the bolder characterizations of their queens. But the evil queen drops out of the other two plays and the tyrant figure becomes less stereotyped in Leontes and Prospero, who are complexly vivid characters. Inversely, Miranda is a much simpler heroine than Imogen or Perdita (and Hermione) or even Marina; and the theme of chastity which centers about her actions becomes less complex in *The Tempest*. In the first three plays, each heroine's chastity is tested, but Miranda's chastity is never challenged by slander or adversity within the play's action. Her attitudes toward the world are much simpler and less critical than the others'; and her almost complete innocence suggests the general progression of all the plays toward the rebirth of a new world.

Shakespeare's tragicomic mode renews man's world by educating the characters' powers to see and to understand meaning beyond their own narrow limits. The numerous instances of disguise and the conscious playing of roles emphasize the fact that given identities are continually being tested. No man is his own, as Gonzalo points out, until the community has been renewed. Individual identity depends upon others' perception of it as well as upon the individual's self-knowledge; therefore, a fixed point of view is never adequate for evaluating either one's private self or one's identity in the world. The resolution of each play ratifies the fact that man has a place in the larger community of men. The interdependence of men upon each other manifests itself in several ways, but the most striking is the case of Gonzalo, who has committed no sin, but who has followed his king's command in allowing Prospero's exile. In similar situations, Camillo flees his land, and Pisanio refuses to obey Posthumus' command to murder Imogen. Pisanio, Camillo, and Gonzalo cannot be condemned for acting as they do, yet their innate goodness, which directs them to action, is not sufficient to realize their natures. They depend upon the goodness of their masters in order to be truly themselves. Only when Posthumus, Leontes, and Alonso have repented and have regained their goodness are their subjects able to achieve the fullness of their own identities. The dependence of servants upon their masters and of subjects upon their kings is a reflection of the dependence of man in his similar relationship to Providence. The assurance which Shakespeare's tragicomedies provide is that Providence, unlike men, is fully good and any man may realize his own goodness in relationship to this master if he chooses.

Shakespeare recognizes man's innate resistance to authority, however, at the same time he dramatizes man's desire to have freedom under a controlled order. The plays suggest that although men do not always realize it, absolute independence is not their goal. Men wish to be led, not driven, so that their own choice is a determinant in the plan that ultimately exceeds their own comprehension. This recognition gives Prospero his superior skill in leading his subjects to fulfill his design for renewing their world, and Shakespeare's relationship to his audience finds its most appropriate metaphor in this wise artificer. Prospero's Epilogue is not so much a "farewell to the stage," as Shakespeare's biographers would have it; rather, the Epilogue draws the audience into an imaginative community with the playwright where we share the control and the commitments of his world of wonder.

Appendix A ⸭ THE AUTHORSHIP
OF *PERICLES*

B ecause the first two acts of *Pericles* seem stylistically stiff and dramaturgically clumsy in comparison with Shakespeare's later work, critics often voice their conviction that Shakespeare had little or nothing to do with them. The last three acts of the play contain passages which are "recognizably" Shakespearean, and the dramatic action is more interesting; therefore, the argument runs, Shakespeare probably wrote the last three acts either completely or in large part. F. D. Hoeniger analyzes the problem clearly: "The whole matter is incapable of being finally decided for the simple reason that external evidence is wholly wanting. . . . The view of mixed authorship must needs rely primarily on the general impression of the play's uneven style, part of which looks as if it could have been written only by Shakespeare, and part of which seems like the work of a third-rate writer." [1] In addition, there is the problem of a corrupt text and the possibility that some of the stylistic ineptitudes were caused by different "reporters." [2]

[1] F. D. Hoeniger, Arden edition, *Pericles* (London, 1963), liii. Hoeniger's treatment of the problems of textual corruption and authorship attribution are helpful and thorough.
[2] *Ibid.*, lvi. Philip Edwards, "An Approach to the Problem of *Peri-*

Paul Bertram points out that the problem of collaboration is a psychological obstacle in evaluating plays like *Pericles*, *Henry VIII*, and *The Two Noble Kinsmen* because modern readers tend to discount their artistic value automatically.[3] If one assumes, however, that the play was written by Shakespeare alone, the inclination is to find artistic purpose in what otherwise might be read as clumsy technique. Very few critics have been willing to grant that Shakespeare might have written the more stilted parts of *Pericles*, but G. Wilson Knight makes a point worth considering: "Even the queer scenes seem to grow in power, perhaps because one gets acclimatized. . . . Finally, after a number of re-readings one begins to suspect some especial purpose in the passages of stilted verse." [4]

Indisputably, the first two acts differ from the last three in poetic style and in dramatic excitement; but the suggestion that someone other than Shakespeare wrote the first two acts is not the only reasonable explanation.[5] The action of the play is organic, and scenes in the last three acts draw a great deal of allusive power from parallels to scenes in the first two acts. There is no break in the action to correspond with a break in the style,[6] and it seems reasonable to consider an explanation that ascribes a conscious artistic purpose

---

cles," *Shakespeare Survey*, V (1952), 25–49, argues convincingly for the existence of two reporters.

[3] Paul Bertram, *Shakespeare and "The Two Noble Kinsmen"* (New Brunswick, N.J., 1965).

[4] G. Wilson Knight, *The Crown of Life* (London, 1965), 33.

[5] I say this despite the conviction which critics like J. F. Danby, *Poets on Fortune's Hill* (London, 1952), 87–103, bring to the argument that a collaborator is the only reasonable explanation.

[6] See Northrop Frye, *A Natural Perspective* (New York and London, 1965), 37–38, for his view "'that a critical examination of the structure of a play seldom if ever needs to take any account of speculations about authorship." Frye adds an important note on the fact that collaborated works may create "a distinct and unified personality" as the artistic control.

to the break in style. Chapter II presents such an explanation: the first two acts present a paradigm of action upon which the last three acts elaborate with greater depth. Several critics have demonstrated the similarities between the structure of *Pericles* and of medieval exemplary romance;[7] and the use of an *exemplum* was a popular structural device in medieval narratives. It seems plausible, therefore, to consider that Shakespeare may have attempted to incorporate this narrative device into the dramatic techniques of a play which consciously revises other medieval devices. Without discounting the possibility of collaboration in *Pericles* or the possibility of two reporters, one may view the stylistic differences between the two segments of the play as the result of an artistic experiment. *Pericles* seems to signal the change that was occurring in Shakespeare's choice of a fable and in his presentational methods.

[7] See especially Hoeniger, Arden edition, *Pericles*, lxxxviii–xci; Robert G. Hunter, *Shakespeare and the Comedy of Forgiveness* (New York and London, 1965); and L. G. Salingar, "Time and Art in Shakespeare's Romances," *Renaissance Drama*, IX (1966), 3–35.

Appendix B ✒ THE RELATIONSHIP
OF *HENRY VIII* AND
*THE TWO NOBLE
KINSMEN* TO THE
TRAGICOMEDIES

M any critics include *Henry VIII* and *The Two Noble
Kinsmen* in their consideration of the last plays as
a group.[1] Both of these plays are late (1612–13) and each is
thought to have been written either partly or entirely by
Shakespeare. I have not included them in this study because
the design and the effects of these two plays differ in kind
from the other four, despite the fact that they share in many
of the premises of Shakespeare's "tragicomic action."

Henry VIII seems to be an attempt to use tragicomic
methods upon historic material. As an experiment, it differs
from *Cymbeline* because its history is recent and lends itself
less readily to mythic form than *Cymbeline*'s history, which
is remote. G. Wilson Knight considers *Henry VIII* to be
the "crown" of Shakespeare's lifework because it defines the
"indwelling spirit of his nation" and "that greater peace . . .

[1] G. Wilson Knight concludes *The Crown of Life* (London, 1965)
with a study of *Henry VIII*. Frank Kermode includes, although sketchily,
The Two Noble Kinsmen in his essay *Shakespeare: The Final Plays*
(London, 1963). E. C. Pettet finds the latter play to be very much a part
of Shakespeare's development of the romance tradition; see Pettet, *Shakespeare and the Romance Tradition* (London, 1949), 162–99. The most
comprehensive study of *The Two Noble Kinsmen*, and one which argues
for Shakespeare's single authorship, is Paul Bertram's *Shakespeare and
"The Two Noble Kinsmen"* (New Brunswick, N.J., 1965).

184

whose cause that nation was, and is, to serve." [2] Knight's enthusiasm for the national vision of *Henry VIII* colors his evaluation of the play's dramatic art; and he finds it a more "satisfying" play than *The Tempest* because *Henry VIII* has "a less visionary and enigmatic conclusion." [3]

The visions of *The Tempest* are hardly as free-floating as Knight suggests, however. They are metaphoric, but the metaphors are clearly correlated with life at the actual level on which it is lived. On the other hand, there seems to be a divorce between the actual and metaphoric levels in *Henry VIII*, primarily because the pattern of the fall of innately noble persons carries a burden over into the happy resolution, which Cranmer's prophecy does not entirely dispel. Knight suggests that despite the waste of potential in the three sacrificed characters (Buckingham, Wolsey, and Katherine), England rises, phoenixlike, out of their destruction. Anne Bullen comes from common stock; Cranmer also rises from the ranks, and his humility contrasts with Wolsey's pride. Both Anne and Cranmer unite with traditional royalty to revitalize England, after the manner suggested in Polixenes' speech in *The Winter's Tale* (IV.iv.92–95). The ritual of the child Elizabeth's baptism, together with Cranmer's prophecy of a prosperous future, thus is meant to override the tragic effects of the earlier parts of the play.

As myth, the play does work this way. But the dramatic force that convinces an audience is missing. Satisfaction seems to be with the intellectual pattern abstracted from the play's action rather than with the enacted drama. *Henry VIII* can be said to resemble the Fletcherian pattern of tragicomedy in emphasizing the emotional oppositions more than the narrative pattern,[4] but the consequences of the three

[2] Knight, *The Crown of Life*, 336.
[3] *Ibid.*, 256.
[4] See Eugene M. Waith, *The Pattern of Tragicomedy in Beaumont and Fletcher* (New Haven, 1952), 118–24.

deaths are more serious than anything in *Philaster* or *A King and No King*. These are, in a very real sense, irrecoverable tragic actions, and the pattern of betrayal established in the first half of the play threatens the harmony of the conclusion, despite the generosity of Buckingham, Wolsey, and Katherine as they approach their deaths. They each die and bless the king, and the accumulation of forgiveness mitigates the king's guilt, but it does not exonerate him. Nor does his support of Cranmer against the council dramatically balance his earlier errors concerning Buckingham and Katherine. As Paul Bertram suggests, the council scene in Act IV shows the king breaking away from Wolsey's influence, which caused Katherine's fall;[5] but, even though it is a reassuring scene, it does not dramatically repair the king's character. This may be due in part to the distance from which we view him at almost every point except in his sorrow at rejecting Katherine (II.iv). In the final acts, ritual is substituted for characterization, and this limits our involvement in the king's renewal. Thus, the difference between *Henry VIII* and the four plays which I have considered as tragicomedies is that in *Henry VIII* ritual is expected to rectify the dramatic action of betrayal:[6] the sense of wonder that all is right in this world is not felt, but only seen and heard. The pageantry and ritual which express a higher destiny for England also release the play from the audience's sense of actuality.

In a different way *The Two Noble Kinsmen* departs from the tragicomic pattern of the four earlier plays. The story is more similar to them in its romance derivation (from Chaucer's *The Knight's Tale*) than to the actual and almost contemporary historic concerns of *Henry VIII*. And there are many moments in which comic and serious impulses qualify

[5] Bertram, *Shakespeare and "The Two Noble Kinsmen,"* 168, 173–76.
[6] Cf. C. L. Barber's comments on the rejection of Falstaff in *2 Henry IV, Shakespeare's Festive Comedy* (Cleveland, 1963), 219.

each other in a tragicomic way. For instance, the interweaving of serious action with the revelation of comically discrepant motives in the first two scenes of Act II is handled with great skill.[7] The Jailer and his daughter's Wooer begin scene one by establishing a marriage contract. The Jailer minimizes his daughter's dowry in a way that suggests he will manipulate the situation according to his own best interests; but the Wooer makes it clear that his interest is in the daughter rather than in the dowry. She enters and all her talk is of the nobility of the attractive prisoners, Palamon and Arcite. The Wooer says with great reserve that "I never saw 'em," and these three leave with the daughter commenting, "It is a holiday to look on them. Lord, the difference of men!" The dialogue then shifts to Palamon and Arcite in the tower, who list complaints about their imprisonment, emphatically contradicting the daughter's assertion that they are "noble sufferers . . . making misery their mirth." They arrive eventually at a state of hyperbolic serenity in which they fashion their prison into a paradise of protective innocence (which reinstates the daughter's opinion—but with an important qualification). They then swear their eternal friendship and Emilia appears below in the garden. Their attitudes change instantly and drastically, and scene two ends with their vows of eternal hatred as the Jailer comes to summon Arcite to his banishment.

This pair of scenes is more than comic because in it are born all the sources of the plot's potentially tragic action. Though we can laugh here at the discrepancy between idealized views of human motives and their experienced contradictions, by the end of the play these issues have become matters for lament. In one sense, this defines the dif-

---

[7] I am following the Regents Renaissance Drama edition of *The Two Noble Kinsmen*, by John Fletcher and William Shakespeare, ed. G. R. Proudfoot (Lincoln, Nebr., 1970).

ference between *The Two Noble Kinsmen* and any of the four tragicomedies.[8] In them, the tragic actions at the beginning of each play seem too threatening for laughter, but by the end of the play we see that our anxiety was unnecessary. In contrast, the situations in *The Two Noble Kinsmen* at the beginning, almost until Act V, seem to promise a happy outcome. When Palamon is saved from death by Arcite's accidental death, there is no release from anxiety, but there is a sorrowful recognition that the gods will have their way despite man's efforts.[9] The point is that the gods' ways are arbitrary and their justice cannot find a satisfactory analogy in the realm of man's action. The fact that Palamon saw Emilia first hardly justifies Arcite's death for loving her too, particularly when Arcite displays magnanimity more frequently than Palamon. It is a strange world that Palamon's final speech describes:

> O cousin,
> That we should things desire, which do cost us
> The loss of our desire! That nought could buy
> Dear love, but loss of dear love!
>
> (V.iv.109–12)

This strangeness is not like the "miracle" of the other plays; in *The Two Noble Kinsmen* the final focus is on justice without mercy, on the sadness of nobility wasted, on the chance which governs man's destiny. Theseus summarizes it: "Never fortune / Did play a subtler game" (V.iv.112–13).

The parallel plot of the Jailer's daughter and her madness that grows out of unrequited love parodically points to the

[8] Cf. Philip Edwards' discussion of the later play's more solemn tone, "On the Design of *The Two Noble Kinsmen*," *Review of English Literature*, V (October, 1964), 89–105.

[9] Pericles' speech following his loss of Thaisa in Act III resembles Theseus' speech which concludes *The Two Noble Kinsmen*. The difference between the two plays is suggested by the positions of these two speeches.

same conclusion. The Wooer disguises himself as Palamon and convinces the daughter that he loves her. Her madness is cured, just as the doctor has predicted in his realistic way (V.ii), and she prepares to wed her Wooer. This resolution of the subplot suggests that love of a particular person is not so important as the fancy suggests. Life has a higher value than the romantic dedication to love, for which Arcite and Palamon have given all.

The methods of *Henry VIII* and *The Two Noble Kinsmen* resemble in many ways those employed in the four tragicomedies, but the vision toward which the technique builds has changed. The change may be implicit in the earlier plays since they resist a total affirmation of the ideal; but "joy" seems to have lost its climactic place in the two later plays.

INDEX

Aeneid. See Virgil

Anachronism: temporal, 45; signal for dislocation, 133

Anderson, Donald K., 151 *n*

Antony and Cleopatra, 3 *n*, 4 *n*, 146 *n*

Anxiety: audience protected from, 49; displaced by comedy, 94, 126, 188; displaced by Prospero, 137–38, 165

Apollo: oracle of, 113, 117, 120, 124, 137

Art: relationship to life, 5, 24–25, 31, 35, 57, 130–31, 165, 185; which displays its art, 6, 16–17; ethical reassessment of, 7; vitality of, 36; improper uses of, 76; limitations of, 165–66, 170

Arthos, John, 43, 54

Artifice: stress on, 5, 6, 7–8, 15, 16, 18, 21, 24, 31–32, 62, 92, 97, 133, 156, 163; distaste for, 6, 25–26; stage, 108; of wonder, 117; of pun, 119; exploded, 120; of analogous structure, 127; of storm, 139; of drawing aside, 163. *See also* Artificiality; Bear; Disguise

Artificiality: stress on, 35, 42; of presenter, 37; of antique form, 39; of choral speech, 61; of disguise convention, 96, 120; of seasonal celebration, 130

Audience: experiences of, 5, 33, 48, 57, 59–60, 110, 112, 113, 128, 156–57, 159; released from sympathy, 5, 128; exploitation of, 7; awareness of, 7, 15–16, 21, 63, 109, 129; in kinship with playwright, 16, 18–19, 29, 137, 174, 177; embarrassed by artificial, 25–26; responses of, channeled, 52, 126; expectations of, 62; modern, 175

Authority: obligations of, 20, 164, 169; submission to, 60, 179; resistance to, 154

Awareness: contradictory, 7, 16–18, 57–58, 63, 93, 120, 176; double, 7, 16 18, 63, 133, 156; of advance knowledge, 57; of roles, 106, 178. *See also* Audience

Balance: of tragicomedy, 17, 22–23, 74, 93, 117, 120, 125, 160; of characterization, 117, 161, 162, 167; emotional, 126

Banquet: in *Pericles,* 41, 58; in *The Tempest,* 149–50, 160, 167

Barber, C. L., 132 *n*, 186 *n*

Barroll, J. Leeds, 3 *n*, 4 *n*, 10 *n*

Bear: in *The Winter's Tale,* 5, 17, 125–27

Beaumont, Francis, 14 *n*, 26–32, 185

Bentley, G. E., 10

Bertram, Paul, 182, 184 *n*, 186

Bethell, S. L., 15, 106 *n*, 111 *n*, 120 *n*, 125 *n*, 127 *n*, 128 *n*

Biggins, Dennis, 125 *n*

Blend: of comedy and tragedy, 54, 90, 93, 117, 125

Bohemia, 5, 125 and *n*

Burckhardt, Sigurd, 33 *n*

Catharsis: of tragicomedy, 14, 23, 58

Catullus, 77

Cause and effect: rationale of, 20 *n*, 49, 51, 85–86, 104, 135

191